Praise for *HOW TO B*
By Engr. Ri

"This book is simply brillian
foundational aspects of hoι
happiness and success. We share the same advocacy of prospering with purpose, which is why I have genuine admiration and respect for the author of this book. Highly recommended!"*
  -JOHN RODICA, Best Selling Author of
  8 Simple Tips for Young Entrepreneurs

"Engr. Rich Magpantay has written a terrific helpful book on how we can become a millionaire. This is complete instruction on how we can set ourselves to succeed in every aspect of our dreams. I recommend this book to everyone who has the willingness and tenacity to overcome challenges to realize their goal. Don't be let out in the road to becoming a millionaire… buy this book now!"
  -JULIE COX, Best Selling Author of
  I Ordered My Future Yesterday

"Thank you, Rich. I admire you for your book and your desire to help Filipinos become wealthy. Your book will bless a lot of people!"
  -SHA NACINO, Best Selling Author of
  Money & Me

"The book has inspired me to believe in the power of dreams and making them happen."
  -MARILYN CERZO, Founder of
  Wisdom Valley Educational Systems, Inc.

Praise for *HOW TO BECOME A MILLIONAIRE?*
By Engr. Rich Magpantay

"A must read book... very informative and a practical guide. Actually, I found it not just merely a book but a vessel of realization of our dreams to come true, the turning way point of everyone else to navigate their money to right track and the light house that serves as beacon to reckon, leading to become a millionaire. Sending SOS (Save Our Savings) to all seafarers around the world to end the old way of being a one day millionaire but to become a millionaire forever."
-Captain GERALD SAMARTINO, *Master Mariner*

"Hi Rich, Congratulations! Being a well-travelled author of the book, you've been searching for the missing link of simple ways of how to become a millionaire. Thank you for sharing with me the ideas on how to do the circulation of my financial success; not only that, but the entire aspects of our lives on how to become wealthy... More power! May the Divine creator bless you more, and the Universe will response in everything you want to be, to have and to do in life... I'm so proud of you!"
-GELYN VALENZUELA, *Miss Money Magnet*

"Great day Rich, Congratulations and thank you for sharing your book. I enjoyed and appreciated your work. This can really help and guide people to attract wealth and happiness. With this book we can make to the TOP!"
-TOPPER REYES, Network Leader of
JM Ocean Avenue

"Hello Rich! Thank you for having this book that you wrote. It really helps me a lot in enhancing my knowledge regarding how to become a millionaire not only for money but for the attitude of pursuing another goal and at the same time helping people."
-EFREN RILLERA, Chief Engineer of *MV Asian Sun*

HOW TO BECOME A MILLIONAIRE?

The Eight Effective Steps of Becoming Successful and Wealthy in All Aspects of Your Life

ENGR. RICH MAGPANTAY
Designer of Equal Prosperity in the World

INTERNATIONAL EDITION

HOW TO BECOME A MILLIONAIRE?

The Eight Effective Steps of Becoming Successful
and Wealthy in All Aspects of Your Life

ISBN 978-971-011-865-6

ENGR. RICH MAGPANTAY

INTERNATIONAL EDITION

Philippine Copyright © 2014 by Arjay M. Magpantay

All rights reserved, including the right of reproduction
in whole or in part in any form.

First printing: September 2014

Translated by Ms. Marilyn Cerzo
Edited by Ms. Bianca Louise Garcia
Cover Design by Engr. Rich Magpantay

Published by

CENTRAL BOOK SUPPLY INC.
927 Phoenix Building, Quezon Avenue, Quezon City
www.central.com.ph

MILLIONAIRE PUBLISHING SOLUTION
Balibago Complex, Santa Rosa City, Laguna
www.howtobecomeamillionaire.ph

ACKNOWLEDGEMENTS

This book is dedicated greatly for you as you step up to become a millionaire. I admire you!

The millions of people who supported me in producing this book: author friends, inspirational speakers, success coaches, wealth mentors, investment advocates, business founders, financial advisors, bank managers, real estate brokers, forex traders, stock market traders, network marketers, leading politicians, celebrity artists, police officers, maritime crews, book editors, graphic designers, software developers, franchise owners, motivational teachers, diligent students, hard-working employees, business partners, family relatives, successful and wealthy persons I have interviewed. I appreciate all of you!

I honor all Filipino men and women around the world who dreams of becoming the greatest person to ever live on Earth, and makes effective steps in achieving them every day. I am inspired daily because of you!

Most of all, I dedicate this book as a gift to my loving wife, *Jayreen*, to my happy sons, *Raven* and *Ritch*, and to *God* to whom I owe my grateful life.

Thank you, thank you, thank you!

INSPIRATIONAL QUOTE

"All successful people men and women are big dreamers. They imagine what their future could be, ideal in every respect, and then they work every day toward their distant vision, that goal or purpose."
— BRIAN TRACY, Author of *Maximum Achievement*

CONTENTS

Acknowledgements	v
Foreword	xi
About the Author	xiii
Introduction: Think Like a Millionaire	**15**
Awaken a Millionaire Eagle	15
Think Like a Millionaire	16
Millionaires of the World	16
A Millionaire Begins in the Mind	17
A Millionaire Starts Today	17
How to Become a Millionaire?	18
Step 1: The Millionaire's Mind	**21**
The Power of the Mind	21
Story of Positive Thinking	23
The Genuine Talent	23
Eight Ways to Awaken your Genuine Talent	24
My Genuine Talent	25
Examples of the Genuine Talent	28
What is your Genuine Talent?	30
What is your Life Purpose?	31
Inspirational Quotes about the Mind	32
The Millionaire's Mind	33
First Millionaire Training	34
Step 2: The Millionaire's Dream	**35**
The Precise Dream	35
Eight Ways to Create your Precise Dream	36
The Precise Dream Technique	37
Example of the Precise Dream	38
The Universal Dreams	39
Everyone is Born Successful	42
Everyone is Naturally Diligent	43
Inspirational Quotes about Dream	44
The Millionaire's Dream	45
Second Millionaire Training	46

Step 3: The Millionaire's Law — 47

- The Universal Laws — 47
- The Law of Attraction — 48
- The Law of Gratitude — 49
- The Law of Success — 49
- The Law of Giving — 49
- The Law of Life — 50
- The Law of Direction — 50
- The Law of Seven — 51
- The Golden Rule — 51
- Inspirational Quotes about Law — 52
- The Millionaire's Law — 53
- Third Millionaire Training — 54

Step 4: The Millionaire's Wealth — 55

- The Purpose of Wealth — 55
- God Wants you to be Happy — 55
- Why you Need to Become Wealthy? — 56
- What do Truly Wealthy People Have? — 56
- What are the Qualities of the Truly Wealthy? — 57
- People who are Above 65 Years Old — 58
- Friends with the Truly Wealthy — 59
- Inspirational Quotes about Wealth — 60
- The Millionaire's Wealth — 61
- Fourth Millionaire Training — 62

Step 5: The Millionaire's Income — 63

- The Massive Income — 63
- We All Have 24 Hours to Earn — 63
- Financial Status — 64
- Story of the Jeepney Driver and Henry Sy — 64
- Start Small and Dream Big — 65
- Handling your Finances Perfectly — 66
- Example of Handling Finances Perfectly — 70
- Inspirational Quotes about Income — 71
- The Millionaire's Income — 72
- Fifth Millionaire Training — 73

Step 6: The Millionaire's Investment — 75

- The Investment Strategy — 75
- Story of the Rat Cyclist — 75
- Making your Investment Grow — 76
- Reading Books — 77
- Attending Trainings — 78
- Saving in Banks — 79
- Engaging in Network Marketing — 80
- Investing in Stock Market — 81
- Investing in Mutual Funds and UITF — 82
- Trading in Forex Market — 83
- Selling Real Estate Property — 83
- Selling Insurances — 84
- Selling Memorials — 84
- Selling Automobiles — 85
- Leasing Houses — 85
- Engaging in a Franchising Business — 86
- Being an Investor — 86
- Learning the Business — 87
- Inspirational Quotes about Investment — 88
- The Millionaire's Investment — 89
- Sixth Millionaire Training — 90

Step 7: The Millionaire's Business — 91

- The Creative Business — 91
- The Creative Product and Service — 92
- Starting Small — 96
- Story of One Peso — 96
- Story of my Classmate — 97
- Richest People in the Philippines for 2014 — 98
- The Richest People are Business Owners — 100
- Why Do Filipino-Chinese Engage in Business? — 100
- Opening a Start-up Business — 101
- Example of Start-up Business — 103
- Managing your Business Profit Perfectly — 105
- Example of Managing your Business Profit Perfectly — 109
- Business Planning — 110
- Example of Five Year Business Planning — 111
- Inspirational Quotes about Business — 114
- The Millionaire's Business — 115
- Seventh Millionaire Training — 116

Step 8: The Millionaire's Habit — 119

- The Powerful Habit — 119
- Story of the Number 28 — 120
- The Grand Mission — 120
- Creator of the World's Powerful Millionaire Prayer — 121
- The Millionaire Prayer — 122
- Eight Statements of the Millionaire Prayer — 122
- Example of the Millionaire Prayer — 124
- Declaring the Millionaire Prayer — 126
- Your 28 Days' Activities of Success and Wealth — 127
- Inspirational Quotes about Habit — 138
- The Millionaire's Habit — 139
- Eighth Millionaire Training — 140

Journey: Start Becoming a Millionaire Now — 143

- The Consistent Praying — 143
- Journey of Becoming a Millionaire — 143
- Taking Small Steps Toward Success — 144
- Becoming a Millionaire Now — 145
- The World's Successful and Wealthy People — 145
- The Two Verses of Truth — 146
- Let your SMART Dreams Come — 147
- Your Millionaire Journey — 148
- Grateful Request — 149
- Success Quote — 150

Richmind Investment Guide — 151

- Success Books — 151
- Financial Trainings — 152
- Network Marketing Companies — 153
- Forex Market Brokers — 153
- Saving and Commercial Banks — 154
- Stock Market Online Brokers — 154
- UITF Companies — 154
- Mutual Fund Companies — 155
- Real Estate Developer Companies — 155
- Insurance Companies — 156
- Pre-need Companies — 156
- Car Dealers — 156
- Franchising Business — 157
- Disclaimer — 158

FOREWORD

ACCEPTANCE

Wealthcome to the world of millionaires!

Good day my friend! Thank you for accepting this millionaire book. I feel inspired that I could serve a great person like you through this book.

This book is your personal property and you have the pleasure to write your thoughts, beliefs, vocabulary, values, rules, references and ideas on every page you desire. This book aims to enlighten the wisdom of the eight effective steps of becoming successful and wealthy in all aspects of your life.

You can bring this book anywhere you go so you can share it with your loved ones. I believe that you will make it a habit to read this book every day and every night, which will serve as your guide as you take on your journey. If you are ready to take that first step toward success, just affix your signature on this book as a symbol of your commitment to achieve your dreams.

Full Name: _____
Date: _____
Signature: _____

OPENING OF THE MIND

Before I explain the eight effective steps of becoming a millionaire, I would like to ask for the openness of your mind to the new knowledge and information that I will share in this book. Understanding the wisdom of these facts and truths would be easier if you would keep an open mind as you read through this book.

PRINCIPLE OF THE EMPTY CUP

A cup's usefulness is in its emptiness. We can't put in more water to a cup that is already full; the water will just spill out of the cup. It's the same thing with our mind. When we are full of ideas, we will not learn something new. I would like to challenge you to "empty" your mind of all pre-conceived thoughts so that you would be able to understand the wisdom that I am about to share with you now.

PURPOSE OF THE BOOK

Why I wrote the book is very simple. I have a great vision that I am helping more than 1 billion people around the world of becoming successful and wealthy using the eight effective steps that I have discovered. Being a millionaire becomes valuable if you are happy, loving, and grateful in all aspects of your life: emotional, intellectual, spiritual, physical, and financial. Success and wealth starts with these effective steps. Let us now begin your journey.

Be the greatest person to ever live,

ENGR. RICH MAGPANTAY

ABOUT THE AUTHOR

ENGR. RICH MAGPANTAY, *Designer of Equal Prosperity in the World*, is a great person who started a simple life before he achieved his dream of becoming successful, one step at a time. He started his humble beginnings in the province of Bicol as a vendor and studied in Manila, Philippines, because of his desire to find a good job.

At an early age, he would always ask why the wealthy becomes wealthier, and what qualities they have. As he moved from one job to another, as he climbed his professional career, and as he travelled around the six continents of the world—Asia, Europe, North America, Australia, Africa and South Africa, and from his interactions with several people of various cultures, he found the answers to his questions. He eventually learned about the secrets of achieving genuine success and true wealth.

He followed every step to achieve wealth and evaluate himself from time to time with the help of the people who are already successful and wealthy. He discovered that an ordinary person can eventually become a millionaire after 28 consecutive days of conditioning his or her mind. He also realized that everything that happens in our lives is part of God's plan for us to achieve prosperity and abundance.

Today, Engr. Rich Magpantay has become one of the famous authors and trainers on success and wealth in the Philippines because of his dream to make every Filipino a happy, loving, and grateful millionaire in all aspects of their lives: emotional, intellectual, spiritual, physical, and financial. He is the creator of the world's powerful millionaire prayer.

Aside from his love for writing and sharing his experiences on achieving wealth, he is also a successful electronics engineer. He wrote two maritime training books that aim to help seafaring professionals become competent in handling cargoes at sea. He also loves reading books about successful and wealthy people. He is lovingly married with two happy sons and a grateful believer of God.

In this book, he shared his years of wisdom that he learned from his own experiences, lessons from his interactions with people of distinctive cultures, and knowledge from working for various companies. Such great wisdom is what brought him to his genuine success and true wealth today.

INTRODUCTION
THINK LIKE A MILLIONAIRE

"Reading not only is as essential as breathing, but just as I have experienced, it will also lead to many exciting passages marked with success."
-SOCORRO RAMOS, Founder of *National Bookstore*

MILLIONAIRE
Truly Wealthy: a genuinely successful person who earns one million pesos or more every month.
- Definition by ENGR. RICH MAGPANTAY

AWAKEN A MILLIONAIRE EAGLE

Through reading, I have learned lessons that helped me in developing my wisdom in achieving success and wealth. Among those that I have read is about the story of an eagle.

An eagle once laid eggs on a tree. Unfortunately, one of the eggs fell on the ground and landed on a bunch of goose eggs. After several days, the eagle's egg hatched together with the goose eggs. The unfortunate eaglet eventually grew up thinking and acting like the geese in the field. One day, the young eagle saw a grown-up eagle flying high over the fields. He wanted to fly like that eagle and so he began to stretch his wings and took off the ground. Before he knew it, the young eagle was soaring and flying high in the sky. His genuine identity was awakened by what he saw.

Most of us are like that young eagle—we are all born "**eagles**" or "**millionaires**". Unfortunately, we are easily influenced by what we see around us, like most of the people living in the Philippines. Living a simple life used to be my lifestyle until I realized that I needed to find an inspiration—someone I can look up to, someone who is successful and wealthy. I believe that if you can find that great person, your millionaire eagle would also be awakened.

THINK LIKE A MILLIONAIRE

As I was going through the list of the richest people in the Philippines for August 2014, I was inspired when I learned that the youngest Filipino millionaire is only 37 years old! He is Edgar "Injap" Sia II, founder of *Mang Inasal*, one of the fastest growing chains of restaurants in the country today. His dream to serve delicious charcoal-grilled chicken to every Filipino paved the way for his success as one of the richest men in the Philippines. That is how a millionaire thinks—by serving millions of people.

MILLIONAIRES OF THE WORLD

Here is the record of the millionaires of the world:

Top Celebrity Stars - Singers, Actors, Athlete	1%
Top Salesmen	5%
Top Specialist – Doctors, Lawyers	10%
Top Executives of Mega Corporations	10%
Businessmen	74%

Source: "8 Secrets of the Truly Rich" by Bo Sanchez

From the record, we can see that a high percentage of businessmen become millionaires. I realized that I do not need to become a heartthrob like Daniel Padilla, or be an excellent actor like Jericho Rosales, or a super boxer like Manny Pacquiao, or academically excellent like doctors and lawyers to become a millionaire. Businessmen become millionaires because they allow all possibilities to happen and continue to pursue their passion for their businesses.

A MILLIONAIRE BEGINS IN THE MIND

It all begins in the mind. I know many people who have become millionaires despite not being able to complete their education or not being able to achieve academic excellence. I saw one thing in common among them—they had the dream to help millions of people. That dream fuelled their passion to learn more to make their businesses succeed. They endured years of determination for their businesses until they reached their goal of becoming millionaires.

A MILLIONAIRE STARTS TODAY

This book contains all the information you need so you can become a millionaire. Once you learn all the knowledge and apply it in your everyday living, you will start living like a millionaire. Let your dreams come your way by doing the eight effective steps of becoming successful and wealthy in all aspects of your life. And it all starts today.

HOW TO BECOME A MILLIONAIRE?

In the next pages of the book, I will share to you the wisdom of the eight effective steps of becoming a millionaire that can help you achieve your dreams faster.

The first step is about the millionaire's mind, which shows the power of positive thinking and in awaking your genuine talent.

The second step is about the millionaire's dream, which illustrates the precise dreams and making your universal dreams come true.

The third step is about the millionaire's law, which enlightens the universal guidelines that you can follow to achieve prosperity and abundance.

The fourth step is about the millionaire's wealth, which clarifies the good attitudes towards prosperity.

The fifth step is about the millionaire's income, which proves that, whether you're an employee or a business-owner, you will be able to gain true wealth.

The sixth step is about the millionaire's investment, which explains the ways to make your knowledge and wealth grow.

The seventh step is about the millionaire's business, which discusses the various businesses of truly wealthy people.

The eight step is about the millionaire's habit, which demonstrates the 28 days' activities to become genuinely successful.

At the end of reading this millionaire book, writing your goals and taking actions on your dreams, you will be able to achieve your goal of becoming successful and wealthy in all aspects of your life: emotional, intellectual, spiritual, physical, and financial aspects faster.

Let us now begin your journey to the first step of becoming a millionaire on the following page...

MILLIONAIRE INTRODUCTION

"A millionaire thinks of serving millions of people."
-ENGR. RICH MAGPANTAY

STEP 1
THE MILLIONAIRES MIND

"Whatever the mind of man can conceive and believe, it can achieve."
-NAPOLEON HILL, Author of *Think and Grow Rich*

MIND
Thinking: Consciousness of a person where the desires, emotions, understanding, beliefs, creativity, and genuine talent comes from, and contains experiences and knowledge.
-Definition by ENGR. RICH MAGPANTAY

THE POWER OF THE MIND

Your mind is the first powerful asset that you have because it can achieve everything you believe in. Positive thinking is very important if you want to make all your dreams come true. You can achieve your dreams only if you are happy from within, if you love the people around you and if you are grateful to God.

A Happy Mind

Everything that comes into our lives becomes attractive when we have a happy mind. With a happy mind, we can have the power to turn things around when things are not going the way we expect them to be. That is why I always say, I am happy for everything that happens to me in every moment of my life.

A Loving Mind

My mind becomes loving when I think of the people I value most – my loving spouse, my cheerful children, my supportive parents, and all the great people around me. If all people will have a loving mind, life on Earth is beautiful because everyone will become a blessing to others. That is why I always say, I am a loving husband, father, son and friend.

A Grateful Mind

A grateful mind can help you in making your dreams come true. People who are full of gratitude are those who receive more blessings. God blesses those who are grateful for everything that is happening in their lives. For instance, every time I hear my child play loudly, I am thankful because my child can speak. I'm thankful when my wife lovingly corrects me at times because it means we are still living together and that we truly care to each other. A pile of unclean laundry means we have clothes to wear. Roads that need repair? Be thankful because it means there are jobs waiting for people. That is why I always say, I am grateful to God for everything I have in my life.

STORY OF POSITIVE THINKING

The mind is a powerful tool if it is used in a positive way. The story of Napoleon Hill's son, Blair, inspired me to use positive thinking. Blair was born without ears. Doctors told the American author that it would be impossible for Blair to hear, thus he would never learn how to speak. Despite the medical facts, Napoleon Hill was determined for Blair to hear. From his son's infancy, Napoleon would always think that the child could hear and speak like normal children. As years went by, Napoleon discovered that 65% of his son's hearing ability was restored. Like normal people of his age, Blair eventually finished his schooling through the help of a company that provided him with a special type of hearing aid, which completed the remaining 35% of his hearing ability.

This story proves that it is very important for our children to hear our positive words and dreams for them so that they would become aware of the beauty of life as they grow up. That is why I always say, I should think positively, and I use positive words as much as I can.

THE GENUINE TALENT

I am grateful for my passion of reading because, through this, I have learned many lessons about positive thinking that I now use every day. This knowledge became my inspiration for creating the concept of genuine talent. The "**genuine talent**" is a God-given gift that can be used to serve people. Having genuine talent could only come from practicing positive thinking, which can be manifested through our emotions and experiences in life.

Using your genuine talent can help you to come up with new ways to make your daily activities easier or create new things that could serve many people happily.

EIGHT WAYS TO AWAKEN YOUR GENUINE TALENT

There eight ways to awaken your genuine talent:
1. Inspiration
2. Love
3. Fame
4. Music
5. Friendship
6. Cooperation
7. Memorable experience
8. Prayer

I learned these eight ways to awaken your genuine talent as written on the book *Think and Grow Rich* by Napoleon Hill - widely considered to be one of the great writers on success topics with estimated 70 million sales of the book. Of the eight, having an inspiration for a great person is the top reason why a person begins to dream. To develop your talent, it is significant for you to receive encouraging response from your loved ones, and to become famous. It is also great for you to listen to inspirational music such as the sound of nature or instrumentals. Through friendship and cooperation, you can gain great ideas that can help you make better decisions. On the other hand, your memorable experiences provide you with various lessons that will help you change your life for the better. Finally, praying consistently can ultimately help you to enlighten your genuine talent. With all these eight ways present in your life, the "**creative genius"** within you will be awakened.

MY GENUINE TALENT

I am "**optimistic and intelligent**", and that is my genuine talent. I act on a positive approach in every situation. I recognized that I am able to awaken my intelligent mind during my third year in high school, when I became the top student in our class at *Bicol Institute of Science and Technology*. It was something new to me that time because I did not excel in grade school. I was really inspired to study that time because I wanted to be noticed by the apple of my eye. She was the reason why I was able to awaken my genuine talent. My inspiration gave me so much happiness, which made it possible for me to easily understand everything my teachers taught me.

Since then, I have continued to show my genuine talent. When I was an Electronics Engineering student at *Mapua Institute of Technology*, I often heard people in our school say that whoever pursues such degree with passing grade in all subjects can be called a *genius*. When I heard this, I became more inspired to pursue my studies. I strived even harder in college so that I could get a good job someday. For five years, I was able to pass all my subjects in college and became an academic scholar.

After college, I became a professional Electrical Engineer onboard the ship *MV Mell Shepherd*. I wondered how I could use my genuine talent to help people. It was on that ship when I started writing this book. The ship became my guide in using my genuine talent. I believe that everything we see and all of our experiences are signs from God that He sends to help us discover our genuine talent.

Developing My Genuine Talent

My experiences and activities that make me happy help me to develop my genuine talent more. The experiences that I have shared about being on top of my class confirmed my genuine talent as an intelligent man. I continued to cultivate my intelligence when I started idolizing Dr. Jose Rizal, our national hero. Like Rizal, I also began reading books. I soon discovered that reading gives me so much pleasure. I love reading biographies of successful and wealthy people. Buying new books to read at our local bookstore makes me happy. Moreover, I was so happy when I finished writing two maritime books for seafarers like me to help them become competent with the proper handling of cargoes onboard. I believe all of these experiences strengthened my genuine talent on "**passion for books**".

My Name and Genuine Talent

Like what I have mentioned previously, all my experiences contained God-given symbols that helped me to use my genuine talent. For instance, my nickname *Rich* means a person who is prosperous; while my last name *Magpantay*, a Filipino language, means equality. My profession as *engineer* means a designer. Together, my name collectively means "**Designer of Equal Prosperity in the World**".

Dr. Jose Rizal is the hero of my life. He wrote *Noli Me Tangere* and *El Filibusterismo* – two great literary works that rekindled the spirit of nationality among Filipinos during the Spanish Era. These books inspired me on how can I help my countrymen to go through a successful and wealthy life.

The initials of the names of my loved ones - my loving wife and cheerful sons - are "RJ", which could also represent "Rizal, Jose". Coincidence? I don't think so.

Using My Genuine Talent

I was able to use my genuine talent as being intelligent, optimistic in life and passionate on books by writing a book, *How to Become a Millionaire?*. Through this, I was able to provide wisdom on eight effective steps that people may use for becoming successful and wealthy in all aspects of their lives – emotional, intellectual, spiritual, physical, and financial. It aims to give inspiration to many people for them to see the achievement of their dreams. It also aims to give hope to millions of people to have a good life through positive thinking and developing belief in their talent.

EXAMPLES OF THE GENUINE TALENT

There have been instances wherein I was able to help people discover their genuine talents by asking questions about their good qualities and what makes them happy. I would usually share my experiences to other people so that they would also learn to discover and use their genuine talent. Aside from being intelligent and optimistic in life, my other God-given gift is my ability to help people use their genuine talent to become successful and wealthy.

One day, my colleague onboard, Ferdie, shared to me that he finds pleasure in watching how bread is made. He likes bread so much and *ensaymada* is his favorite type of bread. Aside from bread, he also loves chocolates. He said he is interested in business but he doesn't know what kind of business to start with. I told him that if he really wants to become successful in business, he would have to start with something that he really loves doing and something that will make him happy. I suggested for him to make the best chocolate *ensaymada*, since I believe, this is his God-given gift.

My other colleague on board, Romy, once shared that he loves watching action movies and I can see that he has a talent for fashion because he has his own style of wearing his glasses every single day. He loves watching drama series on television. I told him that he could be the next action star. All he needs to do is to develop his skills in acting, dancing, and singing so he could become a famous actor.

Mike told me that he loves walking along the fields and that he loves planting rice. His dream is for every person to eat delicious rice at an affordable price, and that children would grow up strong and healthy from eating such rice. He said he likes to have a rice field and his favorite color is green. I advised him to use his genuine talent to develop a variety of affordable "**herbal rice**" that could provide more nourishment for the body, which could be his key to success.

Rey shared once that during vacation, he loves to make wall painting from cardboard cut-outs. His paintings are about nature and that he is very happy doing wall paintings for his local church during special occasions. He is also good at painting with nature as his favorite subject. I advised him to use his genuine talent in creative arts to make wall paintings using native materials to create his masterpieces.

Joseph told me that during his vacation, he makes roasted pig and sells it in retail to his neighbors. I could see his passion for roasting. Aside from roasting, he also loves barbecue. I advised him to use his genuine talent for cooking to start up a small restaurant that would serve the best-tasting roasted pork barbecue in town.

Bert once shared that he loves growing orchids and going to special occasions. I told him that he could start a business in selling orchids as decorations for special occasions.

Jayreen, my loving wife, told me that she loves baking cakes, and that her favorite fruit and perfume scent is strawberry. I advised her to start a pastry business by making the best strawberry cake, which could be the key to her success and fortune.

I was able to help people to discover their genuine talent, which they can also use to serve other people. If you want to succeed and prosper, all you need to do is to use your genuine talent to serve others and to have a great passion for what you always love to do.

WHAT IS YOUR GENUINE TALENT?

To discover your genuine talent, you may ask yourself the following questions:
1. What are my positive experiences?
2. What are the things that make me happy?
3. What activities make me happy?
4. What work am I willing to do even without compensation?
5. What are my good characteristics?
6. According to other people, what are my good characteristics?
7. What place makes me happy?
8. Who are the successful people I know?

WHAT IS YOUR LIFE PURPOSE?

In my life's journey, I discovered that the purpose of man's existence is for him to use his God-given genuine talent to serve others. Through these genuine talents, one will be able to innovate ways and create new things that will make life happier and better. It would be great if you will be able to awaken and discover your genuine talent for the love of others.

The use of your genuine talent to serve others is the beginning of your journey of having a successful and wealthy life. Like Henry Sy who served others by providing thousands of jobs to Filipinos through *SM malls*; Soccorro Ramos who established *National Bookstore* which paved the way for Filipinos to have access to books; Edgar Sia who served others by serving delicious grilled chicken at *Mang Inasal* branches all over the country; Bo Sanchez who shares the gospel and founded *The Feast* which is now hailed as one of the happiest places in the world - all of these millionaires, and all the other millionaires, have all started in their unwavering service to other people. Let these people become our inspiration.

After you have completed the first step of discovering your millionaire's mind, your second step will be...

INSPIRATIONAL QUOTES ABOUT THE MIND

"The starting point of great success in your life begins, in the simplest terms, when you discipline yourself to think and talk about only the things you want and refuse to think and talk about anything you don't want."
— BRIAN TRACY, Author of *Reinvention*

"The single most powerful asset we all have is our mind. If it is trained well, it can create enormous wealth in what seems to be an instant."
- ROBERT KIYOSAKI, Author of *Rich Dad Poor Dad*

"Attitude is the first quality that marks the successful man. If he has a positive attitude and is a positive thinker, who likes challenges and difficult situations, then he has half his success achieved."
— JOHN MAXWELL, Author of *The Success Journey*

"The purpose of our lives is to add value to the people of this generation and those that follow."
— T. HARV EKER, Author of *Secrets of Millionaires Mind*

"I remember as a little boy I ate one meal a day and sometimes slept in the street. I will never forget that and it inspires me to fight hard, stay strong and remember all the people of my country, trying to achieve better for themselves."
-MANNY PACQUIAO, *8-Division World Boxing Champion*

"Countrymen: I have given proofs, as well as the best of you, of desiring liberty for our country, and I continue to desire it.
— JOSE RIZAL, *Philippine National Hero*

"Think big! You are going to be thinking anyway, so think big!"
—DONALD TRUMP, Author of *Why We Want You To Be Rich*

THE MILLIONAIRE'S MIND

"The positive thinking of a man awakes the genuine talent that can be used to serve millions of people."
-ENGR. RICH MAGPANTAY

The first step of becoming a millionaire is to have the millionaire's mind through happiness, loving others, gratitude to God and positive thinking. Through positive thinking, you can discover your God-given genuine talent that you can use to serve people, which is the reason for your life purpose. Your genuine talent can be awaken through inspiration, love, fame, music, friendship, cooperation, memorable experiences and prayer. Using your genuine talent to serve other people is the first step for you to become successful and wealthy in all aspects of your life.

FIRST MILLIONAIRE TRAINING

I. Who is your greatest inspiration in life?
   1.

II. What are the eight ways for you to awaken your genuine talent?
   1.
   2.
   3.
   4.
   5.
   6.
   7.
   8.

III. Discover your genuine talent through these questions:
   1. What are my positive experiences?

   2. What are the things that make me happy?

   3. What activities make me happy?

   4. What work am I willing to do even without compensation?

   5. What are my good characteristics?

   6. According to other people, what are my good characteristics?

   7. What place makes me happy?

   8. Who are the successful people I know?

STEP 2
THE MILLIONAIRE'S DREAM

"All our dreams can come true, if we have the courage to pursue them."
- WALT DISNEY, Creator of *Disneyland*

DREAM
Desire: Written goal of a person that he or she wants to become, things that he or she wants to have or activities that he or she wants to do to be able to have a better and happier life.
-Definition by ENGR. RICH MAGPANTAY

THE PRECISE DREAM

It is very important for a person to have a dream. I have dreamed of becoming a millionaire, and it is also my dream to help my fellow Filipinos to become successful and wealthy. In the second step, I will explain what would make a precise dream for it to become a reality. This step is related with the book, *Think and Grow Rich* by Napoleon Hill (1937) – a research book that was written based on analyzing more than 25,000 rich people over a span of 25 years.

Most people have dreams of becoming rich but not everyone knows how much wealth he or she wants to have. Their dream of becoming rich does not come true simply because their dreams are not precise. In this step, you will learn how to make precise dreams for them to come true.

EIGHT WAYS TO CREATE YOUR PRECISE DREAM

There are eight ways to create your precise dream:
1. What do you want to have?
2. When do you want to have it?
3. What will you do to earn it?
4. What do you want to become?
5. Write your goals.
6. Affix your signature on that goal.
7. Read this goal every morning.
8. Read this goal every night.

What Do You Want to Have?

It does not matter how much the dream is worth. As long you know the exact amount that you dream of, you just need to believe it will come true.

When Do You Want to Have It?

It is essential for you to know when or on what specific date the dream will become a reality.

What Will You Do To Earn It?

It is important for you to know what activities you should do to achieve that dream.

What Do You Want to Become?

You need to find out how you will improve yourself and develop your character so that you can reach that dream.

Write Your Goals

Write the exact amount, specific date, activities and character to achieve your precise dream on a paper.

Affix Your Signature

Affix your signature on the paper as a symbol of your commitment to your goals.

Read Your Goal Every Morning and Every Night

You have to make sure that you read the written goals that you have made twice a day – upon waking up in the morning and before you sleep at night. It is important for you to declare your precise dreams every day and every night so that it will always be in your mind. It is also essential for you to feel the greatness in your heart every time you read your dream so that it will always inspire you to do what you have conditioned yourself to do.

THE PRECISE DREAM TECHNIQUE

Andrew Carnegie used to be an ordinary steel worker in America until he used this technique to build his dreams to succeed. Since using this technique, he was able to earn more than 100 million dollars! He eventually shared this technique of having precise dreams to Napoleon Hill.

EXAMPLE OF THE PRECISE DREAM

Using this technique, I am able to create my own precise dream. Utilizing my genuine talent, which is being intelligent and optimistic in life, and being passionate about books, I was able to come up with my precise dream:

1. What to have: Php 1,000,000
2. When: Today until December 1, 2015
3. What to do: Write the book, *How to Become a Millionaire?*
4. What to be: Become a famous author
5. Write the goals: "I am happy that I am earning Php 1,000,000 beginning today until December 1, 2015. I love writing the book *How to Become a Millionaire?.* I am grateful that I am becoming a famous author sharing more than one million copies of this book in the entire Philippines. All Filipinos who reads this book is becoming happy, loving and grateful millionaire in all aspects of their lives – emotional, intellectual, spiritual, physical, and financial."
6. I affixed my signature on my written goal.
7. Every morning when I wake up, I declare this goal with great feeling.
8. Every night before I go to sleep, I declare this goal with great feeling.

THE UNIVERSAL DREAMS

Aside from having precise dream for your life in one year, it is also important to have universal dreams for all aspects of your life: emotional feeling towards other people and nature, intellectual capability, spiritual state, physical health and financial stability.

Dream to Serve Millions of People

I dream of serving millions of people using my genuine talent by writing this book and be able to help more people to become successful and wealthy in all aspects of their lives. Ask this to yourself, "What are my dreams in life so that I could serve millions of people?"

Dream to Become More Loving to Others

My dream of becoming more loving to others, especially to my family, paved the way for the success I desired. Loving people attract their dreams because of their overflowing affection for others. I wrote this book so that more people will learn to love their families more and the people around them. Ask this to yourself, "What do I have to do so that I can be more loving to others?"

Dream to Become More Nature-loving

Your dream to become more loving to the environment, such as the animals, eagles, fish, trees, flowers, plants, clouds, wind, mountains, fields, rivers, seas, and everything that has life, is an essential key in achieving your dreams to become prosperous. If you will think about it, it is our nature that provides for everything that we need for us to achieve our goals. Ask this to yourself, "What do I have to do so that I can be more loving towards nature?"

Dream to Become More Successful

I also looked for successful people who will inspire me. I learned from their humble beginnings, and I discovered how they became successful. In my journey of becoming successful, I met Robert Kiyosaki, best-selling author of *Rich Dad Poor Dad*. He has written over 15 books which have combined sales of over 26 million copies. I call him my Rich Dad because of the life-changing lessons he taught me about becoming wealthy. He served as my inspiration as a father. I have always longed for a father since my father already went to heaven when I was only seven years old. I have always looked for a person who will teach me how to become wealthy until I met Rich Dad. Rich Dad taught me the right way of handling my finances through his books. I also got the idea to share all my wisdom about building wealth through writing books. He served as my inspiration to become a famous author. Ask yourself, "Who is my mentor to become successful?"

Dream to Do What You Want to

I had dreamed before of writing a book, investing in stock market, UITF, forex trading, real estate, and insurance, engaging in network marketing, taking a vacation in Hong Kong and Davao City with my family, and travelling to six continents of the world. I was able to achieve all these because I purposely desired for it with my mind and believed with my heart. Ask yourself, "What are the things that I have always dreamed of doing?"

Dream to be Grateful

Being thankful to God is very important if you want to have a good spiritual state in life. I believe that everything that happens in my life is a blessing from God, and these blessings will be my stepping stones in achieving the success and wealth I desire. Being grateful is the key to your success. You are alive because of God, and He gives you all the desires you need. Ask yourself, "What do I need to do to be grateful to God?"

Dream to Have Good Health

I also desire to become healthy in the physical aspect of my life by having an attractive body. When we are healthy, we feel much better. As the saying goes, *"Heath is Wealth"*, that is why I practice self-discipline by eating fruits and vegetables, drinking clean water, exercising daily, and choosing to be happy. I also noticed that having a healthy lifestyle is also a key to self-healing. Ask yourself, "What do I have to do to have a healthy lifestyle?"

Dream to Have What You Always Wanted

I used to dream of having a house and car each worth more than Php 1,000,000. I strived to achieve these dreams and after several years, I was able to turn these dreams into reality. I realized that having precise dreams gives direction to our lives, especially if we know how much we need to earn to get that precise dream. Life is like a ship. If you know where you're headed, you'll surely get there. I believe that if you have a precise dream, you will surely come up with ways to get that written goal. Ask yourself, "What are those things that I have always dreamed of having?"

EVERYONE IS BORN SUCCESSFUL

I believe that every person was born to become successful. Even before a baby is born, one sperm cell had succeeded out of millions to fertilize one egg cell in the mother's womb. Even before you were born, you are already successful. You are the result of that successful sperm! If you will reflect on this, it means that all your dreams are bound to come true because you have always been successful even before you were born.

EVERYONE IS NATURALLY DILIGENT

I believe that every person is naturally diligent. It only happens that we meet people who are not diligent probably because they are not inspired to dream. I believe that if I will be able to inspire someone, I am certain that this person will become diligent and that he or she will do everything to reach his or her precise dream.

After you have completed the second step of writing your millionaire's dream, your third step will be...

INSPIRATIONAL QUOTES ABOUT DREAM

"The number one reason most people don't get what they want is that they don't know what they want."
– T. HARV EKER, Author of *Secrets of the Millionaire Mind*

"Man must form a clear and definite mental image of the things he wishes to have, to do, or to become; and he must hold this mental image in his thoughts, while being deeply grateful to the Supreme that all his desires are granted to him. The man who wishes to get rich must spend his leisure hours in contemplating his Vision, and in earnest thanksgiving that the reality is being given to him."
– WALLACE WATTLES, Author of *The Science of Getting Rich*

"A man who acquires the ability to take full possession of his own mind may take possession of anything else to which he is justly entitled."
— ANDREW CARNEGIE, Founder of *Carnegie Steel Company*

"Committing your goals to paper increases the likelihood of your achieving them by one thousand percent."
— BRIAN TRACY, Author of *Maximum Achievement*

"The size of your success is measured by the strength of your desire; the size of your dream; and how you handle disappointment along the way."
- ROBERT KIYOSAKI, Author of *Retire Young Retire Rich*

"The more you see yourself as what you'd like to become, and act as if, what you want is already there, the more you'll activate those dormant forces that will collaborate to transform your dream into your reality."
-DR. WAYNE DYER, Author of *The Power of Intention*

"You have to have a dream, whether big or small, then plan, focus, work hard and be very determined to achieve your goals."
-HENRY SY, Founder of *SM Malls*

THE MILLIONAIRE'S DREAM

"The precise dream gives direction into your life for you to become successful and wealthy."
-ENGR. RICH MAGPANTAY

The second step of becoming a millionaire is writing your millionaire's dream. There are eight ways to create your precise dream. It is essential to know the exact amount, the specific date to have it, activities to do, character to develop, write your goals, affix your signature on it and declare it with a great feeling upon waking up in the morning and before you go to sleep at night. It is necessary to have universal dreams of becoming successful and wealthy in all aspects of your life – emotional, intellectual, spiritual, physical, and financial.

SECOND MILLIONAIRE TRAINING

1. Write up your precise dream in life one year from now.
   i.
   ii.
   iii.
   iv.
   v.
   vi.
   vii.
   viii.

2. Write up your dream to serve millions of people.

3. Write up your dream to be more loving to other people.

4. Write up your dream to be more loving to nature.

5. Write up your dream to be more successful.

6. Write up your dream to become grateful to God.

7. Write up your dream to achieve good physical health.

8. Write up your dream to have what you always wanted.

STEP 3
THE MILLIONAIRE'S LAW

"Wisdom is the child of integrity—being integrated around principles. And integrity is the child of humility and courage. In fact, you could say that humility is the mother of all virtues because humility acknowledges that there are natural laws or principles that govern the universe."
-STEPHEN COVEY, Author of
The 7 Habits of Highly Effective People

LAW
Rules: Guidelines that a person must follow in order to achieve prosperity and abundance.
-Definition by ENGR. RICH MAGPANTAY

THE UNIVERSAL LAWS

Through reading, I discovered that there are many rules that I can use as guidelines to help me achieve my precise dream of becoming successful and wealthy. Because of these lessons, I learned to evaluate my actions to determine whether these actions will be in accordance to the universal laws that I have found to be effective in achieving my written goals. These universal laws govern to all people on Earth, whether you are good or not. Learning these universal laws will help you to achieve your precise dream faster and effective.

THE LAW OF ATTRACTION

The Law of Attraction states that what we think will positively happen. Everything that we ever thought about will happen because this is according to this law. If you think that you are living a good life, then all the good things will come to you. If you believe that you have all the things you wanted—that you're driving your dream car or you're living in your dream home—the Law of Attraction will make it possible for you to achieve your dreams. The only thing needed for your dreams to come true is to feel happy, loving and grateful in every moment of your life.

Before I became a successful Electronics Engineer, I studied and self-reviewed for the board exam for 28 days. I believed that I would pass the examination. I had a happy feeling about it that I even went to the movie I love a day before the exam. Before I took the exam, I went to Quiapo church, Santa Cruz church and Baclaran church to thank God. The Law of Attraction was the key to my success in passing the board exam to become an Electronics Engineer.

You would notice that most of the words that I used in this book are positive ones because I believe that every word we express reflects our personality. I want to use positive words all the time so that it will also yield positive results in my life.

Remember, what you think will positively happen.

THE LAW OF GRATITUDE

The Law of Gratitude states that giving thanks will result to receiving. This means that every time you sincerely say thank you to what have you received, the more success will come your way.

Remember, say thank you every moment.

THE LAW OF SUCCESS

The Law of Success states that we need to serve other people to become successful. Our purpose in life is to serve others by creating something new from our God-given genuine talent.

Remember, serve more people with passion.

THE LAW OF GIVING

The Law of Giving states that we need to give our help to others. Setting aside a ten percent part of our income as charity enables us to help the unfortunate people, those who are in need, and the churches. Through giving, I believe that you will receive prosperity, which may also come in other forms such as job promotion, more customers, higher sales, business profits and greater wisdom.

Remember, give your help to the needy people, church and charity.

THE LAW OF LIFE

The Law of Life states that we owe our lives to God. I believe that my life comes from God and that He can take it back anytime according to His plan. At the end of my life, I will leave the legacy I have to those I love especially my family. This realization taught me what matters most in life. I learned to be grateful for everything I have and the life that I am enjoying now. I realized that I have to give more time for my family and loved ones because they are the reason why I live today.

Remember, live a great life with your family and loved ones.

THE LAW OF DIRECTION

The Law of Direction states that dreams give direction to a person's life. This direction will help you reach your success because you will know what you need to do to achieve your goals. Like a ship's voyage, it is carefully planned so that it reaches its destination at the right time and at the right place.

Remember, proper direction guides you towards your success.

THE LAW OF SEVEN

The Law of Seven states that a person's mind pattern changes every seven days or every week. On the first week, you will learn a new lesson. Then, you use these new lessons on the second week. After which, you evaluate your actions based on the lessons you used on the third week. Then, you come up with good decisions based on the lessons you used if these actions fit on you on the fourth week. After the fourth week, you will act on these new lessons repeatedly. Through this law, I discovered that it would take 28 consecutive days for a person to totally change his or her believe from a new lesson.

Remember, for 28 consecutive days, your beliefs will transform into new wisdom.

THE GOLDEN RULE

The Golden Rule states that: do unto others what you want others to do unto you. If you want to be treated by others as a great person, treat others as the greatest person to ever live and make your day as the greatest day you have ever had.

Remember, respect everyone you meet.

After you have completed the third step of remembering all of the millionaires law, your fourth step will be...

INSPIRATIONAL QUOTES ABOUT LAW

"If you want to find greater happiness and fulfillment in your life, you must begin to understand and live in harmony with the law of attraction."
— JACK CANFIELD, Author of *The Success Principles*

"Whoever has gratitude will be given more, and he or she will have an abundance. Whoever does not have gratitude, even what he or she has will be taken from him or her."
-RHONDA BYRNE, Author of *The Magic*

"Success in life depends upon happiness, and happiness is found in no other way than through service that is rendered in a spirit of love."
— NAPOLEON HILL, Author of *Law of Success*

"It's not how much we give but how much love we put into giving."
-MOTHER TERESA, Author of *The Joy in Loving*

"Success is... knowing your purpose in life, growing to reach your maximum potential, and sowing seeds that benefit others."
-JOHN MAXWELL, Author of *How Successful People Think*

"Movement in a new direction helps you find new cheese."
— DR. SPENCER JOHNSON, Author of *Who Moved My Cheese?*

"The practices are designed to be completed over 28 consecutive days. This allows you to make gratitude a habit and a new way of life. Practicing gratitude in a concentrated effort over consecutive days guarantees that you will see the magic take place in your life – and fast!"
-RHONDA BYRNE, Author of *The Magic*

"Do unto others what you want done unto you."
— CONFUCIUS, Author of *The Great Learning*

THE MILLIONAIRE'S LAW

"There are universal laws that will guide you to prosperity and abundance."
-ENGR. RICH MAGPANTAY

The third step of becoming a millionaire is remembering all of the millionaire's laws. These universal laws of prosperity and abundance are the Law of Attraction, Law of Gratitude, Law of Success, Law of Giving, Law of Life, Law of Direction, Law of Seven and the Golden Rule.

THIRD MILLIONAIRE TRAINING

1. What is the Law of Attraction?

2. What is the Law of Gratitude?

3. What is the Law of Success?

4. What is the Law of Giving?

5. What is the Law of Life?

6. What is the Law of Direction?

7. What is the Law of Seven?

8. What is the Golden Rule?

STEP 4
THE MILLIONAIRE'S WEALTH

"If God gives a man wealth and property and lets him enjoy them, he should be grateful and enjoy what he has worked for. It is a gift from God."
– ECCLESIASTES 5:19

WEALTH
Treasure: Property of a person that has value.
-Definition by ENGR. RICH MAGPANTAY

THE PURPOSE OF WEALTH

The purpose of wealth on this world is to give happiness to the people we love, we help and we serve. It is valuable to use our treasures to help people who are in need, the church and charity in order to live a meaningful life. I realized that if you will be able to help others, you will be remembered for the good that you have done.

GOD WANTS YOU TO BE HAPPY

God wants every person to be happy. I believe this is the reason why you are able to show your love for your family, enjoy every delicious meal, have access to clean water, do whatever you want in life, be surrounded by good things, travel to beautiful places, buy whatever you want, develop your positive view, create new things and help others. God wants you to have everything you want to become wealthy in all aspects of your life. God provides for everything you need in this world; however, you need to ask this from Him so that you can live happier. Ask and you will receive.

WHY DO YOU NEED TO BECOME WEALTHY?

You need to be wealthy so that you can help the unfortunate people, give tithes to the church and give donations to charity. Helping others has truly inspired me in life. When you help your church, you are grateful that more people will be able to hear the Word of God. When you give donations to charity, you know that you are helping to provide food, medicines, jobs and houses to those who are in need. By giving help, you know you are giving hope to people to also have a prosperous life.

WHAT DO TRULY WEALTHY PEOPLE HAVE?

Since I was a child, I have always wanted to become wealthy. At a young age, I usually ask our simple community on how I can become wealthy. They said that the wealthy people have big salaries to spend on whatever they want for elegant houses, stylish cars and fashionable things. They also said that I would need to study well so that I will be able to get a good job after graduation.

I told myself that I needed to find a good job so that I can have everything that the wealthy people have. That was until I met Robert Kiyosaki, *New York Time's* best-selling author for *Rich Dad Poor Dad*, who transformed my mind into establishing my own business instead. Through reading the book he wrote, he explained that the truly wealthy people are those who are engaged in big businesses. These businesses provide for their massive income, elegant houses, stylish cars and fashionable items. I realized that owning big businesses is the reason why the wealthy becomes wealthier. Since then, I am inspired every day; I even started my own business so that I can also live like the truly wealthy.

WHAT ARE THE QUALITIES OF THE TRULY WEALTHY?

I learned a lot about the good qualities of the truly wealthy because of the financial trainings that I have attended. I discovered that the truly wealthy have three valuable qualities:
1. Using their genuine talent to persuade
2. Valuing time: earning even while on vacation
3. Having precise dreams

I was grateful when I learned these valuable qualities because they are distinct from what I had in my mind when I was younger. From the trainer, I learned how the truly wealthy use these qualities to their success.

According to the financial trainer, the truly wealthy are constantly developing new ways of using their genuine talents to come up with strategies and plans to help their businesses grow. They also have the ability to persuade others to cooperate with their vision. A truly wealthy person also earns while on vacation. His business will still run even if he or she is on a vacation because he or she has people working for him or her who will follow a certain system or procedure to ensure that every worker does his or her job well. The truly wealthy have a precise dream or a written goal which gives the business direction. They place the picture of their precise dreams on the green vision board where they can always see it and they are being reminded every day about the written goal they plan. They love color green as it symbolize prosperity, peacefulness, enlightenment, nature, abundance, success and wealth. The truly wealthy use this technique to achieve their precise dreams.

Because of these valuable qualities of the truly wealthy, I discovered what characteristics you need to develop to become successful and wealthy in your life.

PEOPLE WHO ARE ABOVE 65 YEARS OLD

The following record reveals the current financial status of people who are above 65 years old in the Philippines:

40%	Have to keep on working to survive
30%	Depend on their relatives to survive
20%	Depend on their SSS or GSIS pension
8%	Depend on charitable institutions
2%	Are financially independent

Source: "8 Secrets of the Truly Rich" by Bo Sanchez

The record shows that only 2% who are above 65 years old are truly wealthy in the Philippines, who chose to use their genuine talents while they were still young to serve other people. I realized that it would be a great choice to use your genuine talent now to serve others so that before you reach the age of 65, you will be earning 1 million pesos or more every month even if you are on happy vacation with your family.

FRIENDS WITH THE TRULY WEALTHY

As the quote says, "*Birds of the same feather flock together*", we attract people who are like us. I had a life-changing experience that proved the meaning of this saying in my life.

When I was younger, I didn't know anything about liquor until I met my college friends who taught me how to drink liquor. When I graduated from school and landed on a job, my colleagues were into singing and they taught me how to sing. When I was on board a ship, my co-workers taught me to play computer games like DOTA. When I began reading books about successful and wealthy people, I learned to live a successful and prosperous life, and be with people who are also interested in building wealth.

I realized how simple it is to have true wealth: be associated with the truly wealthy to discover what they do to build wealth. Through their help, you will learn their best business practices like upgrading the quality of products, establishing harmonious relationship with employees, engaging in humanitarian efforts, and proper management.

After you have completed the fourth step of realizing the purpose of the millionaire's wealth, your fifth step will be...

INSPIRATIONAL QUOTES ABOUT WEALTH

"I've always believed that we, as individuals, have to be the change that we dream of. We all have the hero within us and we can unleash it by coming together uniting for a common purpose for the sake of our country, our community, our very own family."
- EFREN PENAFLORIDA, *2009 CNN Hero of the Year*

"Life isn't about trying to be expert in everything. It's about being expert in one thing and offering it to the world."
—BO SANCHEZ, Author of *You Have the Power to Create Love*

"As a nation, we also desire peace and prosperity for our region and for the rest of the world: the foundation of progress for all."
—BENIGNO AQUINO III, *President of the Philippines*

"Give a man a fish, feed home for a day. Teach a man to fish, feed for a lifetime."
— CONFUCIUS, Author of *The Great Learning*

"I'm very happy to see the people... This victory is not just for me. This is a victory for the Filipinos as well."
—MEGAN YOUNG, *Miss World 2013*

"An asset is something that puts money in my pocket. A liability is something that takes money out of my pocket."
- ROBERT KIYOSAKI, Author of *Cashflow Quadrant*

"You are the average of the five people you spend the most time with."
— JIM ROHN, Author of *My Philosophy for Successful Living*

"Thoughts become things. If you see it in your mind, you will hold it in your hand."
— BOB PROCTOR, Author of *You Were Born Rich*

THE MILLIONAIRE'S WEALTH

"The purpose of wealth on this world is meaningful for helping people who are in need, for church and for charity."
-ENGR. RICH MAGPANTAY

The fourth step of becoming a millionaire is realizing the purpose of your millionaire's wealth. Your wealth is made meaningful through helping people who are less fortunate, tithing to church and donating to charity. God wants you to become wealthy so you can have a better and happier life. Learning the valuable qualities and associating with the truly wealthy paves the way of becoming successful and wealthy.

FOURTH MILLIONAIRE TRAINING

1. How can I give help to those people in need?

2. Who is the person that I know needs help?

3. How can I help the church?

4. To which church will I give my tithes?

5. How can I give my help to charity?

6. To which charity will I give my donations?

7. Among those I know, who are the truly wealthy?

8. What are the three valuable qualities of the truly wealthy?
    i.
    ii.
    iii.

STEP 5
THE MILLIONAIRE'S INCOME

"Your income can grow only to the extent that you do."
— T. HARV EKER, Author of *Secrets of Millionaire's Mind*

INCOME
Earning: Amount received by a person based on his or her work or through investment.
-Definition by ENGR. RICH MAGPANTAY

THE MASSIVE INCOME

Each person has his or her own way of earning, either through employment or through business. The distinction in your income mainly depends on what you do to achieve the level of massive income you want or on your perseverance to continue what you have started in your career. Which of the two will actually make a person truly wealthy – employment or business?

WE ALL HAVE 24 HOURS TO EARN

Everyone has twenty-four hours to earn in a day. However, others can earn one million pesos in a day while others could not earn even a single peso in a day. The reason behind this is relatively simple: the one who earns one million pesos has big dreams and strives to increase his or her earnings through the use of God-given genuine talent. How much do you earn every month?

FINANCIAL STATUS

The table shows what I believe is the financial status of a person depending on monthly income that he or she received:

Person Status	Monthly Income
Not-rich	Php 28,000 and lower
Average	Php 29,000 to 99,000
Comfortable	Php 100,000 to 900,000
Rich	Php 1,000,000 to 9,000,000
Very Rich	Php 10,000,000 and more

We can tell whether a person is rich or not based on his or her monthly income. I use this to evaluate and determine your financial status. Once you become fully aware of this, then you start working on your dream to become a rich person or a millionaire.

STORY OF THE JEEPNEY DRIVER AND HENRY SY

Let me tell you a story about the jeepney driver and Henry Sy. The jeepney driver represents the self-employed while Henry Sy represents the business owner. They both have 24 hours to work in a day. The jeepney driver wakes up early in the morning to prepare his jeepney for the day ahead. He starts driving in the morning to make sure he will get more passengers throughout the day, and he usually goes home late at night. While driving, he also multi -tasks: calling the passengers and accepting payments from passengers. He does this routine every single day. We could say that he is hard-working but his income will only depend on the number of passengers that would get on his jeepney.

How about Henry Sy, being a business owner? He does not need to work physically on his business since he already established a systematic procedure. In his chain of SM Malls, he delegates people who will manage his business. Each of his employees follows a system to ensure that the business processes work orderly. Henry Sy has provided jobs to many Filipinos through his chain of malls in the entire country, that is why he was cited by *Forbes* as the richest Filipino as of August 2014. But before he became successful, he first became a vendor of selling shoes in Quiapo. Can you imagine how the dream of this business tycoon started with only a pair of shoes?

START SMALL AND DREAM BIG

Many of the branding names we know today started out as small, motivated businesses. Behind these businesses are smart working people who dared to dream big like Henry Sy, Socorro Ramos, Edgar Sia and Bo Sanchez who used their God-given genuine talents in helping people.

Henry Sy, who first came to the Philippines at age 12, started his humble beginnings selling shoes in Quiapo. He is now known as the no.1 richest man in the Philippines for his chain of *SM Malls* in the entire country with an estimated net worth of $12.7 billion.

Socorro Ramos, together with her husband, started selling books in Avenida after World War II. Through her ingenuity, she has transformed the bookstore into the largest chain in the country today, *National Bookstore*.

Edgar Sia II opened the first *Mang Inasal* store on December 2003. After seven years of operation, his stores rose to 306 branches. Now he holds the 31st spot in the list of richest men in the Philippines in August 2014 at the age of only 37 years old.

Bo Sanchez used to have a small Bible and a wooden rosary in his hands. Now he has become a successful businessman, motivational speaker and best-selling author. He also started a spiritual community called *Light of Jesus*.

These successful people started with simple lives by handling their monthly income properly in order to start a small business. They live below their means and follow a technique of handling finances the perfect way.

HANDLING YOUR FINANCES PERFECTLY

To handle your monthly income the perfect way, consider the following table as your guide in coming up with your financial accounting:

Love Account	1%
Vacation Account	4%
Happy Account	5%
Giving Account	10%
Investing Account	10%
Responsibilities	70% or lower
Total Income	**100%**

Income for the Love Account

The income for the love account (1%) is the amount you are going to provide as an inheritance for the people you love. In this way, you know that your family is safe by the time you leave this world because you have properly saved up for their future in the bank. This also serves as a symbol of love to all your perseverance and success in life.

Income for Vacation Account

You will only use this account for vacation (4%) when you are no longer working. Through this amount, you can visit beautiful places in the Philippines and see the rest of the world. You can also buy anything you want after years of working. You can also take vacations with your family and you can have the ability to buy for them whatever they desire through this income allocated for vacations.

Income for Happy Account

The income for happy account (5%) is the amount that you are spending every month for buying whatever you want or for doing activities with your family as a reward for all your work in every month. You won't be able to tell when is the time you will leave the Earth, so it's better to choose to spend quality time with your family. You have to make them feel that they are more valuable than your work because they are the reason why you are working.

Income for Giving Account

The income for giving (10%) is the amount you use to give help to those unfortunate people, tithes for church and donations for charity. The law of giving is a rule of universe that you must remember and follow if you want to be successful and prosperous. When you give to people who are in need such as your parents, siblings, relatives, or people on the streets, you become a channel of prosperity to the world. Through giving, you know that you will be remembered by the good deed you've done. Giving tithes to the church shows your faith in God, and you know that this is also a way for you to achieve your dreams faster. Giving donations to charity also helps you to get what you want in life because you are reaching out to those in need.

Income for Investing Account

The income for investing account (10%) is the amount that you use for developing your knowledge and building your wealth for the business that you will start. You use this as a guide so that you can meet the people who will help you in making your business succeed. You can learn many things about investing that you can use for establishing your own business. You can actually earn more from stock market, mutual funds, unit investment trust funds, forex trading, real estate house rental, bank time deposit, government bonds, insurance, memorials, franchising business, network marketing and other business that I will discuss in the next chapter.

Income for Responsibilities

The income for responsibilities (70%) is the amount you use for paying your obligations such as house rental, car loan, food, clothing, household, utilities such as electricity, water, internet, phone, and cable TV subscription, association dues, tuition fees, allowance, etc. If there will be something left out of it, you will use it in addition to next month's income or to other accounts.

Total Income

Once you practice the self-discipline of using the perfect way to handle your monthly income consistently, I believe that you will certainly become successful and wealthy in all aspects of your life.

EXAMPLE OF HANDLING FINANCES PERFECTLY

Let's say I am earning Php 10,000 every month as an ordinary employee.

Love Account (1%)	Php100
Vacation Account (4%)	Php400
Happy Account (5%)	Php500
Giving Account (10%)	Php1,000
Investing Account (10%)	Php1,000
Responsibilities (70%)	Php7,000 or lower

I will save the percentage of my monthly income for love account of Php100 and the vacation account of Php400 in the bank so that it will be kept safe until the right time comes. I will spend the happy account of Php 500 to buy whatever I desire as a reward for my effort. With Php 1,000, I will give help to the needy, to church and to charity so that I can comply with the law of giving. I will allocate Php 1,000 for investing or to start a small business. The remaining Php 7,000 is what I will pay for food, transportation and for other financial obligations such as electricity, water, telephone, etc. Through this practice, I am successful and wealthy in all aspects of my life.

After you have completed the fifth step of proper handling your millionaire's income, your sixth step will be...

INSPIRATIONAL QUOTES ABOUT INCOME

"Whatever your income, always live below your means."
— THOMAS STANLEY, Author of *The Millionaire Next Door*

"Because you and I have the power to impute beauty on anything under the sun... because you become the labels you give yourself... if you declare you're beautiful – not despite your imperfections, but because of them – then you are."
-BO SANCHEZ, Author of *The Abundance Formula*

"You can have everything in life that you want if you just give enough other people what they want."
— ZIG ZIGLAR, Author of *Born to Win*

"Not everything can be accomplished by intelligence alone. You need perseverance, motivation, and discipline to reach your full potential."
-MIRIAM DEFENSOR SANTIAGO, *Philippine Senator*

"I just trust my instincts, I trust what feels nice, what feels right, what sounds good, what kind of message in a song sounds relevant to Pinoys."
-OGIE ALCASID, *Multi-awarded singer-songwriter*

"Whatever you desire for yourself, affirm it for others, and it will help you both. We reap what we sow. If we send out thoughts of love and health, they return to us like bread cast upon the waters."
-CHARLES HAANEL, Author of *The Master Key System*

"Computers are great because when you're working with them, you get immediate results that let you know if your program works. It's feedback you don't get from many other things."
-BILL GATES, Founder of *Microsoft*

THE MILLIONAIRE'S INCOME

"Your massive income is proportional to the millions of people you help."
-ENGR. RICH MAGPANTAY

The fifth step of becoming a millionaire is proper handling of your millionaire's income. To handle your monthly income perfectly, you can use this effective account: 1% for love, 4% for vacation, 5% for happy, 10% for giving, 10% for investing, and 70% or less for responsibilities. By investing a percentage of your monthly income, you can start a small business using your genuine talent in serving people. You will become successful and wealthy in all aspects of your life by following the perfect way of handling your finances.

FIFTH MILLIONAIRE TRAINING

I. The Millionaire's Income
   1. What is your financial status right now?

   2. How much do you earn?

   3. What do you do in 24 hours?

   4. Who do you know earning more than 1 million pesos every month?

   5. What is your work?

   6. Do you love your work?

   7. Do you use your genuine talent in your work?

   8. What kind of small business will you start in order to use your genuine talent in serving people?

II. Handling your monthly income perfectly:

Total Income	Php
Love Account (1%)	Php
Vacation Account (4%)	Php
Happy Account (5%)	Php
Giving Account (10%)	Php
Investing Account (10%)	Php
Responsibilities (70% or less)	Php
Income Left	Php
I will put the income left to	Account

STEP 6
THE MILLIONAIRE'S INVESTMENT

"In any investment, you expect to have fun and make money."
-MICHAEL JORDAN, *Greatest Basketball Player of All Time*

INVESTMENT
Learning: Allocating a person's income for increasing knowledge and building wealth.
-Definition by ENGR. RICH MAGPANTAY

THE INVESTMENT STRATEGY

You need an investment strategy before you are able to start your own business. There are various ways to invest in developing your knowledge and in making your wealth grow depending on your genuine talent or chosen passion. Through investing, you will learn from people you will meet, especially those who acquired a great wisdom in banking, writing books, conducting trainings, engaging in network marketing, stock market, mutual funds, forex trading, real estate, insurance, memorials, car selling, franchising and start-up business.

STORY OF THE RAT CYCLIST

Let me tell you first a story why I am able to open my mind into allocating my monthly income for investing. I was invited to attend a financial education training that aims to change the way people think about making income out of employment. In this training, I heard about the story of the rat cyclist – a rat that continues to run in a mounted wheel inside a cage. As the rat runs, the wheel also turns. No matter how fast the rat runs in the wheel, the rat does not get anywhere and stays where he runs.

And then it hit me. I realized that I was just like that rat. I will work eternally in my life since every time I receive my salary, all my earnings goes into the usual payments for the house, electricity, water, food, car, transportation and communications. If there is anything left out of it, I buy an immediate gratification such as designer clothes, shining jewelry, trendy gadgets and holiday fun. When there is nothing left, I had to work again. It is a continuous cycle. If I keep on doing the rat cycle, I will end up working for the rest of my life!

After hearing about the story of the rat cyclist, I changed the way I think about handling my earnings. I realized that you need to save percentage of your monthly income so that you can prepare for the future of your family and loved ones and be able to take a vacation even if you are no longer working. It is better to save now while you're still young so that you can reap its benefits and you can even retire young and retire a millionaire.

MAKING YOUR INVESTMENT GROW

The first step I took to improve my investment strategy is through financial literacy which is not taught during my school days even in college. In

Philippine education system, the Filipinos are taught to become a great worker or employee and that is the reason why we have plenty of skilled OFW working abroad.

Through the financial literacy I have attended, I learned more about the various ways to make my investment grow. I needed this to determine if I am allocating my earnings on the right investment. I am now able to compare various companies that offer the same products or services for me to know which company is better. I realized that to expand your wisdom in investing, you should learn to read books, attend trainings and you have to start with a small amount and improve how to make it more profitable.

READING BOOKS

Reading books about the success stories of famous people helped me discover the secrets behind their businesses that turned into branding names. Through their experiences, I can learn how to make my business work as they serve as my mentors.

Robert Kiyosaki's books taught me why I need to mind my own business. The wisdom I learned from Rich Dad inspired me to write this book about getting truly wealthy. I also read the success books of Napoleon Hill, a greatest writer about success, so I can learn how to write a best-selling book of all time. Napoleon Hill inspired me to succeed in life and to become a famous author like him.

I realized that while you are reading an inspiring story of successful and wealthy people, listening to instrumental music also helps you to bring out your genuine talent. Remember, continue in developing your wisdom by reading books so you can become genuinely successful, that is why it is good to invest in your personal development.

ATTENDING TRAININGS

In starting out any business, it is essential to attend trainings on the same type of business you're going to create. Many people I have met in the trainings guided me in establishing my start-up business and continue to teach me on intensifying it. Most of the wisdom I know today came from the trainings I attended and the great people I met. I realized that my life experiences are also a great factor to the magnificent wisdom I have today that I am also able to share to you.

In all the trainings that I have attended, I realized that the training would only be effective if you have the right attitude towards learning. Let me share with you some helpful tips when attending trainings. First, it is important to open up your mind to any idea that will be presented during the training. Think of the empty cup principle – the usefulness of the cup is only achieved when it is empty. Clear your mind of any preconceived ideas so that you can learn more. Second, take down notes, so have your notebook and pen ready. Third, always bring your USB flash disk with you. You might want to ask for a copy of the presentation used by the speaker. Fourth, keep all your senses alert so you can learn effectively. The amount of information we learn depends on the mode of learning: 10% when reading, 20% when using diagrams and illustrations, 30% when listening, 70% when sharing what you have learned, 90% when sharing what you have learned and applying it in your real life experience. Fifth, keep on attending trainings. The more you attend, the more you learn. As a rule, repetition is the master of all learning.

Remember, learning from trainings and from your own personal experiences can help you expand your wisdom, thereby you can make better decisions.

SAVING IN BANKS

Allocating your money in the bank is a good venue in making your money grows instead of putting your money inside a bamboo tree or piggy bank. The amount that you are allocating into the bank savings account could earn about 0.25% per year, or 2% per year if you'll put the same amount in time deposit. Interest in time deposit may be earned monthly, quarterly, semi-annually or annually. The investment that you will allocate for this is the income for love account (1%) and for vacation account (4%), as I have discussed previously in the millionaire's income.

Remember, what you will save in the bank is what goes to the inheritance of your loved ones and to your vacations after your retirement.

ENGAGING IN NETWORK MARKETING

One of the choices I had for investing is in network marketing companies. It was good for me to know about how the marketing and selling works so that I can also use this in establishing my own business. Bear in mind, however, that there are things that you need to consider before joining in a network marketing company. First, learn more about the company profile – the number of years it has been existing and its stability as an organization. Second, learn more about the quality and the market price of the products. Third, you should know who will be your team leader that will transform you as a network builder.

Network marketing would only require a small investment but the income it promises for those who work professionally in building network is overflowing. I have seen many people who became successful at doing this business within two years or more. Another feature of network marketing companies is the free personal development trainings they provide for their distributors. I have met people from all walks of life when I engaged in network marketing. Being with them helped me to develop my self-confidence and skills in marketing and selling, which I believe are fundamental qualities of a successful business person.

The initial investment for you to engage in network marketing companies is about Php 4,000 to Php 100,000, depending on the packages you choose from. As much as possible, pay directly to authorized company branch offices to receive the products included in the packages.

INVESTING IN STOCK MARKET

If you want your money to grow over a long period of time, invest in the stock market where you can earn up to 20% per year, depending on the economic status of the country. There are two ways to earn in the stock market: (1) when the price of the stocks you bought increased, and (2) through dividends when the company you chose makes its profit.

There are two types to participate in the stock market – as an investor or as a trader. Let's say you want to be an investor in the stock market. You will buy stocks from a company at a prevailing price in long term. When the company profits, you will receive dividends as a stockholder depending on how many shares you bought. For example, you bought stocks from JFC (Jollibee Foods Corporation). To make sure that you will earn more, you need to consider the various ways of how Jollibee can make more profits. Jollibee earns when more customers are coming in. Therefore, continued patronage of Jollibee products will increase the company's profits. So every time you grab a bite at Jollibee, you know that you are doing your own little way of helping the company to earn because you are also a stockholder.

The other type to participate is to become a trader in the stock market. I have to buy stocks and sell these even in a short period of hours or in less than six months. It requires a lot of skills and talent to determine which stocks are going up or going down in the market. To do this, you have to attend professional stock trader's training so you can learn the fundamentals and technical analysis works.

The live trading in the Philippine Stock Market is open from Monday to Friday, 9:30 a.m. to 12:00 noon, and 1:30 p.m. to 3:30 p.m. The minimum investment is Php 5,000 for investors and Php 25,000 for traders.

INVESTING IN MUTUAL FUNDS AND UNIT INVESTMENT TRUST FUNDS

The Mutual Funds (MF) and Unit Investment Trust Funds (UITF) are offered by companies that invest in the stock market and bonds to people who want to buy stocks or bonds in a diversified portfolio. These two companies differ in terms of ownerships: MF is for private companies and UITF is for banks. Both can yield up to 20% per year depending on the economic status of the country. These funds are also classified as Equity, Balance and Bond. Equity Fund is 100% top blue chip stocks company. Balance is 50% stocks and 50% bonds, while Bonds is 100% government or private company bonds.

The amount of investment you need for such funds ranges from Php 5,000 to Php 25,000. For this type of investment, there is about 2% trust fee every year for the professional fund managers who handle the trading of buy and sell of stocks or bonds.

TRADING IN FOREX MARKET

Trading in foreign exchange (Forex) or currency market requires a great deal of skill and talent. It is highly technical that one needs a clear understanding of terminologies used in this type of trading. Compared to the stock market, this type of investment is highly unsafe because of the fast-changing percentage in point (pip) or currency pair. Successful trades can enable you to earn up to 100% quarterly conservatively.

With a minimum amount of USD 100 to USD 200, you can join the live Forex trading from Monday to Friday.

SELLING REAL ESTATE PROPERTY

Becoming a real estate salesperson can greatly develop your selling skills because it is where you learn how to deal with people. The best thing about it is that you can do this as a "sideline" during your free time after work. Through real estate, you can increase your monthly income. You can earn a commission as a salesperson, which is based on 3% of the total selling price, and as a licensed real estate broker with 5% commission. For instance, if you're able to sell a house and lot worth 1 million pesos, your earning as a salesperson is Php 30,000. But what if you can sell 10 house and lots in a year? That means you can earn a total of Php 300,000 additional income in a year while helping other people have their own homes! Now if you're a licensed real estate broker, you can earn Php

50,000 if you are able to sell a house and lot of the same value.

Before you begin in this type of industry, remember that training is a must. You first have to learn and develop the right kind of skills necessary for you to be able to become genuinely successful.

SELLING INSURANCES

By providing professional advice to people who are interested in getting insurance plans, you can also increase your monthly income as a financial advisor. If you want to engage in this type of industry, you have to attend trainings provided by the insurance company so that you will learn more about their products and its benefits to the plan holders. After you have attended the trainings, then you are now ready to take the licensure examination. Upon passing, you may already sell the insurance plans provided by the company! Just like in selling real estate, this also requires a great deal of skill and talent in communications and public relations. Through this type of job, you can earn up to 10% of the selling price of the insurance plan.

SELLING MEMORIALS

Another way to increase your income is by becoming a memorial lot and service salesperson. Nowadays, people see buying memorial lots as a way of preparation for the unknown. Most of us believe that we owe our lives to God and that anytime He wills, He can take it back. If you want to become successful in this type of business, you have to determine the most persuasive reason for people to buy memorial lots and services. In this type of selling, you can earn up to 7% commission on every lot sold, which means this can increase your monthly income significantly. All you have to do is to develop your communicating skills and public relations.

SELLING AUTOMOBILES

Selling cars and other types of vehicles is also a great way of earning higher income. To become a successful car salesperson, you need to have an idea of the type of car or vehicle that best suits the needs of the customer. This type of business also has a good potential because more and more Filipinos are now buying cars.

LEASING HOUSES

Leasing houses has become a very profitable business nowadays because the population in urban areas is continuously increasing. The best thing about this business is that no extraneous physically work is required of you for you to earn out of it. All you have to do is to ensure that the house is properly maintained. It is also a good idea to have apartments instead of houses because you can offer more units at affordable prices. Having more tenants would yield to greater income.

ENGAGING IN A FRANCHISING BUSINESS

Having a franchising business is a good start for first-time entrepreneurs. Since the business already exists and already has marketing tools, it is now effective to sell the products. All you have to do is to learn how this system works, from managing to marketing up to selling. As a franchisee, the company will be committed in helping you make your business work. As you learn in the process, you will be able to have the opportunity to make the business grow, which is a great stepping stone in eventually putting up your own business.

BEING AN INVESTOR

If you have the capital for investing but don't have the skill to start your own business yet, consider being an investor in a start-up business. Usually, start-up businesses require an initial capital and not all entrepreneurs have sufficient capital to start their businesses. This is where you can play the game. You can provide them with the funds they need in exchange for a certain percentage of their profits. But before you engage in seeding, make sure that you know the type of the proposed business and study the business proposal in detail. Invest only with people that you personally know and trust.

LEARNING THE BUSINESS

The best way to learn everything about the business you want to have is by starting at the bottom – get yourself hired in a company that is in the same line of business you are interested in. This is the most effective way to learn about how the business works – managing people and resources, employee relations, compensation and benefits, planning, financial management, etc. After learning the fundamentals, you will add your own personal experience to establishing your own business using your creativity and genuine talent.

After you have completed the sixth step of allocating your millionaire's investment, your seventh step will be...

INSPIRATIONAL QUOTES ABOUT INVESTMENT

"Don't work for the money; let the money work for you."
- ROBERT KIYOSAKI, Author of *Retire Rich Retire Young*

"Anyone who stops learning is old, whether at twenty or eighty. Anyone who keeps learning stays young. The greatest thing in life is to keep your mind young."
— HENRY FORD, Founder of *Ford*

"Tell me who your heroes are and I'll tell you how you'll turn out to be."
— WARREN BUFFETT, Author of *The Essays of Warren Buffet*

"It is extremely important to have marketing experience in starting a business. This lessens the risk of failure in business because of errors committed out of inexperience. Having a mentor or a business adviser is important too."
-FRANCIS KONG, *one of the Best Motivational Speakers in the Philippines*

"The sooner you start, the faster you learn."
—GIAN JAVELONA, CEO of *OrangeApps*

"Trademark is an important thing. Trademark increases a lot of value to our business."
—TONY TAN CAKTIONG, Founder of *Jollibee*

"More than physical beauty, what I really wanted to emphasize is inner beauty."
—MIRIAM QUIAMBAO, *Miss Universe First Runner-Up 1999*

"Learning the secret of flight from a bird was a good deal like learning the secret of magic from a magician."
— ORVILLE WRIGHT, Creator of *First Flying Plane*

"Through my music, I want to urge children to dream, and dream big."
—APL.DE.AP, Member of Award Winning *Black Eyed Peas Band*

THE MILLIONAIRE'S INVESTMENT

"Your investment strategy is to learn from other companies in establishing your own business."
-ENGR. RICH MAGPANTAY

The sixth step of becoming a millionaire is by allocating your millionaire's investment effectively. There are various ways to grow your investment strategy, starting with: reading books, attending trainings, saving in the bank, engaging in network marketing, investing into stock market, mutual funds, UITF, and forex market, selling real estate, memorial lots, insurance plans, and automobiles, leasing houses, franchising business and becoming an investor in start-up companies. Learn the business by starting at the bottom; getting yourself hired in a company with the same vision as yours.

SIXTH MILLIONAIRE TRAINING

1. How much is your allocation for your investment?

2. Who are the successful investors that you know?

3. What success books do you need to read?

4. What type of financial training do you need to attend?

5. How much have you saved in the bank?

6. Attend a business presentation sponsored by at least three network marketing companies.
7. Attend training about stock market.
8. Look for a private company offering mutual funds as your prospect opportunity for additional income.
9. Ask your bank about investing in UITF.
10. Attend training about forex market trading.
11. Attend training about selling house and lots.
12. Attend training about selling insurance plans.
13. Attend training about selling memorials.
14. Attend training about selling automobiles.
15. Attend training about leasing houses.
16. Attend training about engaging from franchising.
17. Invest in a start-up company owned by someone you know and trust.
18. Be an employee in a company that has the same type of business that you are interested in putting up.

STEP 7
THE MILLIONAIRE'S BUSINESS

"The essence of a successful business is really quite simple. It is your ability to offer a product or service that people will pay for at a price sufficiently above your costs, ideally three or four or five times your cost, thereby giving you a profit that enables you to buy and to offer more products and services."
— BRIAN TRACY, Author of
The 100 Absolutely Unbreakable Laws of Business Success

BUSINESS
Entrepreneur: A creative person or company that produces innovative products or services that help people.
-Definition by ENGR. RICH MAGPANTAY

THE CREATIVE BUSINESS

Being creative in the business is the key to an entrepreneur's success. If you will use your genuine talent, it will give you the edge you need in business. People are longing for changes especially if it will make their lives easier and better. Through your creativity, you can come up with innovative ways to improve an existing product or service, or introduce a new product or service that is not yet in the market.

THE CREATIVE PRODUCT AND SERVICE

Here are several creative products and services that will give you an idea for your start-up business using your genuine passion. Learn to focus on one of the listed product or service when you start your business.

Creative Ideas for Innovative Products

1. Invention of new creative product
2. Delicious baked breads
3. Delicious baked cakes
4. Delicious chicken meat dishes
5. Delicious beef meat dishes
6. Delicious pork meat dishes
7. Delicious seafood dishes
8. Nutritious vegetable dishes
9. Nutritious fruit dishes
10. Nutritious sweet dishes
11. Nutritious fresh egg
12. Owning a farm of healthy chicken
13. Owning a farm of healthy pig
14. Owning a farm of healthy cow
15. Cultivation of healthy seafood
16. Nutritious ice cream
17. Nutritious beverages
18. Nourishing purified water
19. Fascinating fragrances
20. Stylish clothes
21. Stylish shoes
22. Stylish caps
23. Fashionable jewelries
24. Fashionable bags
25. Educational toys
26. Home-grown and beautiful flowers
27. Home-grown and healthy vegetable plants

28. Home-grown and healthy fruit plants
29. Agriculture of herbal rice field
30. Beautiful park view
31. Beautiful water resorts
32. Beautiful children's playground
33. Quality office depot
34. Quality home depot
35. Quality furniture for building
36. Quality furniture for home
37. Quality equipment for automobiles
38. Quality equipment for ships
39. Quality equipment for airplanes
40. Manufacture excellent automobiles
41. Manufacture excellent ship
42. Manufacture excellent airplane
43. Manufacture excellent building
44. Quality enduring paints
45. Efficient and stylish electronic gadgets
46. Efficient and stylish smart phones
47. Efficient and stylish computers
48. Efficient home appliances
49. Effective laundry cleaning
50. Healthy hair products
51. Body products for beauty
52. Body products for wellness
53. Body products for health
54. Relaxing massage spa products
55. Facial beauty products
56. Success story books
57. Financial literacy books
58. Attractive advertising tools
59. Desirable digital printing products
60. Furnish houses for lease
61. Creative business school
62. Innovative investment school
63. Effective exercising equipment
64. Attractive lighting fixture
65. Creative genuine passion product

Creative Career for Professional Services

1. Invention of new creative service
2. Blissful singer
3. Sensational actor
4. Marvelous dancer
5. Fabulous musician
6. Tremendous music band
7. Magnificent movie director
8. Olympic team for basketball
9. Olympic team for football
10. Olympic team for volleyball
11. Olympic athlete for boxing
12. Olympic athlete for bowling
13. Olympic athlete for table tennis
14. Olympic athlete for taekwondo
15. Olympic athlete for badminton
16. Olympic athlete as runner
17. Olympic athlete for billiard
18. Olympic athlete for golf
19. Olympic athlete for karate
20. Best-selling author
21. Best-selling novelist
22. Best-selling poet
23. Effective inspirational speaker
24. Effective financial trainer
25. Effective newscaster
26. Leading politician
27. Chief Executive Officer of a corporation
28. Professional Certified Public Accountant
29. Professional and attractive Marketing Executive
30. Professional and charming Sales Executive
31. Professional Purchasing Officer
32. Professional doctor
33. Professional lawyer
34. Professional architect
35. Professional engineer
36. Professional teacher

37. Professional agriculturist
38. Professional veterinarian
39. Professional nutritionist
40. Professional care-giver
41. Professional machinist
42. Professional police officer
43. Professional army member
44. Professional chef
45. Professional clothes designer
46. Professional electronics designer
47. Professional ship captain
48. Professional ship chief engineer
49. Professional airplane pilot
50. Professional real estate salesperson
51. Professional automobile salesperson
52. Professional insurance counselor
53. Professional memorial counselor
54. Professional stock market trader
55. Professional fund manager
56. Professional network marketing builder
57. Professional forex trader
58. Professional website designer
59. Professional software developer
60. Professional creative choreographer
61. Professional creative painter
62. Professional automobile designer
63. Professional ship designer
64. Professional airplane designer
65. Professional building designer
66. Professional movie scriptwriter
67. Professional world peace maker
68. Professional charitable service provider
69. Professional evangelical service provider
70. Professional clean environmental service provider
71. Professional clean water service provider
72. Professional creative genuine passion career

STARTING SMALL

Many successful entrepreneurs in the country today also started small. When you're in the business, as long as you do it consistently over a long period of time, you wouldn't notice how fast it grows. I believe that having a business is the key to achieving success and wealth in the world. Think about this: from a pair of shoes to *SM Malls* by Henry Sy; from one book to *National Bookstore* by Socorro Ramos; from one grilled chicken to *Mang Inasal* by Edgar Sia; and from one Bible to *Light of Jesus* Community by Bo Sanchez. All these successes and wealth just started with only one humble beginning.

STORY OF ONE PESO

Let me tell you a story of how a single peso could be of great value. Did you know that it is possible to turn one peso to more than 100 million pesos in just 28 days? Because of this thought, I always evaluate so I can invest my single peso wisely. How do you value a single peso?

To have more than 100 million pesos, you need to double the value of your earning every day within 28 days, and you can only achieve it if you will use your genuine talent to come up with a creative product or service that you can share to the world to serve millions of people. Let me illustrate to you how a single peso can turn into more than 100 million pesos.

Day	Pesos
1	1
2	2
3	4
4	8
5	16
6	32
7	64
8	128
9	256
10	512
11	1,024
12	2,048
13	4,096
14	8,192

Day	Pesos
15	16,384
16	32,768
17	65,536
18	131,072
19	262,144
20	524,288
21	1,048,576
22	2,097,152
23	4,194,304
24	8,388,608
25	16,777,216
26	33,554,432
27	67,108,864
28	**134,217,728**

STORY OF MY CLASSMATE

I have a classmate in grade school who became one of my inspirations in establishing my own business using my genuine talent. After graduation in elementary, I haven't seen him. I studied in Manila at *Mapua Institute of Technology* as an engineering student that time in such a prestigious school. I was a DOST scholar for 5 years who passed all subjects with good grades. I became a successful Electronics Engineer after graduating college.

My classmate, on the other hand, was an average student when we were in grade school in Bicol. When I met him again in Quezon City in 2013, he told me what had happened to him after he graduated from college and started out a small printing business. He relied on his genuine talent for persuading people to have their printing jobs given to him. From one person who trusted him with a project, his customer base began to grow, and his digital printing company now has more than 50 employees. Doing his business for only 10 years, he is now earning more than one million pesos in a month.

That experience made me realize that being academically excellent does not guarantee your journey to earning millions. Even a person of average intellect can become rich through establishing their own business.

RICHEST PEOPLE IN THE PHILIPPINES FOR 2014

Net Worth Calculated as of August 2014

Rank	Name	Worth	Age
1	Henry Sy & Family	$12,700 M	89
2	Lucio Tan & Family	$6,100 M	80
3	Enrique Razon, Jr.	$5,200 M	54
4	Andrew Tan	$5,100 M	62
5	John Gokongwei, Jr.	$4,900 M	87
6	David Consunji	$3,900 M	92
7	George Ty & Family	$3,700 M	81
8	Family Aboitiz	$3,600 M	-
9	Jaime Zobel de Ayala & Family	$3,400 M	80
10	Tony Tan Caktiong & Family	$2,000 M	61
11	Robert Coyiuto, Jr.	$1,800 M	61
12	Lucio & Susan Co	$1,700 M	59
13	Emilio Yap	$1,500 M	88
14	Manuel Villar	$1,500 M	64
15	Inigo & Mercedes Zobel	$1,200 M	58
16	Alfredo Yao	$1,000 M	70
17	Andrew Gotianum	$995 M	86
18	Vivian Que Azcona & Family	$935 M	-
19	Eduardo Cojuangco	$870 M	79
20	Beatrice Campos & Family	$825 M	-

21	Ricardo Po & Family	$ 770 M	-
22	Oscar Lopez & Family	$700 M	84
23	Alfonso Yuchengco & Family	$ 685 M	91
24	Roberto Ongpin	$ 680 M	77
25	Betty Ang	$ 670 M	-
26	Dean Lao	$ 625 M	55
27	Manuel Zamora	$ 620 M	74
28	Carlos Chan	$ 550 M	73
29	Jorge Araneta	$ 510 M	-
30	Mariano Tan, Jr.	$ 445 M	52
31	Edgar Sia	$ 390 M	37
32	Ramon Ang	$380 M	60
33	Michael Romero	$ 375 M	41
34	Concepcion Family	$ 320 M	-
35	Philip Ang	$ 315 M	73
36	Frederick Dy	$ 310 M	59
37	Luis Virata	$ 300 M	60
38	Alfredo Ramos & Family	$ 260 M	70
39	Wilfred Steven Uytengsu, Jr. & Family	$ 255 M	52
40	Tomas Alcantara	$ 250 M	68
41	Jose Antonio	$ 240 M	67
42	Bienvenido Tantoco, Sr. & Family	$ 235 M	93
43	Jacinto Ng	$ 230 M	-
44	Gilberto Duavit & Family	$ 200 M	79
45	Menardo Jimenez	$ 195 M	82
46	Eric Recto	$ 190 M	51
47	Walter Brown	$ 183 M	75
48	Felipe Gozon	$ 182 M	74
49	P.J. Lhuillier	$ 180 M	-
50	Juliette Romualdez	$ 170 M	-

Source: www.forbes.com/philippines-billionaires

THE RICHEST PEOPLE ARE BUSINESS OWNERS

From the list of the richest people in the Philippines for 2014, you would notice that most of them are business owners or entrepreneurs. Most of the ones who dominated the list are Filipino-Chinese because they have a different culture and perspective when it comes to business. They engage in business because they were raised to believe that entrepreneurship is the only way to get rich.

If all Filipinos would only think of establishing their own businesses, then I believe that every Filipino will become truly wealthy, and my great vision that all OFW will work here in the Philippines will come true. The meaning of OFW will transform to "**Overseas Foreign Workers**", referring to foreigners from other countries who are working here in the Philippines because Filipinos are becoming wealthy business owners. The Philippines will be called "**The Business Capital in the World**" as what I have dreamed of.

WHY DO FILIPINO-CHINESE ENGAGE IN BUSINESS?

In one of the trainings I've attended, I met a Filipino-Chinese who is the president of a famous company. He shared his story and the reason why Filipino-Chinese engage in business.

According to him, he was taught by his parents at a very young age to study well so that he can become a businessman. Their culture taught them the value of education as the key to their success in the world of business. He said that all the good qualities that are needed to become successful in the business world can be found in most Filipinos. Only one thing is missing – the desire to be an entrepreneur.

That is why the mission of the president of this famous company is to transform the state of mind of Filipinos by encouraging them to start their own businesses and create wealth through entrepreneurship.

OPENING A START-UP BUSINESS

Let me share with you eight simple process to open a start-up business using your genuine talent.
1. Know your genuine talent.
2. Discover how you can help.
3. Think of a good business name.
4. Register under DTI.
5. Start your business.
6. Sell your products or services.
7. Improve your products or services.
8. Expand your market.

Know Your Genuine Talent

The first step in starting out a start-up business is to discover your genuine talent by examining yourself. Ask yourself this question: What are the things that I love doing?

Discover How You Can Help

The next step is to develop how you can use your genuine talent to help others either by creating a product or offering an innovative service. Think of how you can serve more people.

Create a Good Business Name

Think of a good name for your business. It should be catchy but it must sound professional and trustworthy.

Register under DTI

Go to the nearest DTI (Department of Trade and Industry) Office in your area and have your business name registered. If you wish to operate within your barangay, the registration fee is only Php 200. If your business operation is within the city, the registration fee is Php 500.

Start Your Business

Start your business by creating a unique product or by offering a service that has not been offered to the market yet. This way, you won't have any competition in the business yet since it is a unique product.

Sell Your Products or Services

Start with only one customer and then aim to become famous at doing this business. Be motivated and enthusiastic in selling your products or service to anyone that needs it. Focus on the market area in your place.

Improve Your Products or Services

Improve your products or services by listening to customers' feedback. Remember that a business that started with the proper use of God-given genuine talent must be creative enough to serve more people. There is always room for improvement.

Expand Your Business

Once your business is earning massively, plan for its expansion. If your business aims to provide services and aids to others, you may turn it into a non-profit organization. This will help you reduce the cost of business taxes. Have your business registered in the form of Corporations with the Securities and Exchange Commission (SEC), local government and Bureau of Internal Revenue (BIR) to ensure that all your business transactions are legal. This will enable you to expand your business easier.

EXAMPLE OF START-UP BUSINESS

I opened my start-up business using my genuine talent of being intelligent, optimistic in life and passionate for books. I wrote the book entitled *How to Become a Millionaire?*, which features eight effective steps of becoming successful and wealthy in all aspects of your life: emotional, intellectual, spiritual, physical, and financial.

The name of my business is MILLIONAIRE PUBLISHING SOLUTION. I produce books which fall under PUBLISHING. The book is about achieving success and wealth that's why the business name bears the word MILLIONAIRE. I believe that this book will benefit and give SOLUTION to all those ordinary people who want to become millionaires around the world.

I had my business registered under DTI, local government, BIR and SEC to legalize all my business transactions. All the income of my business will be used to pay the salaries of the people working and business expansion. The language I used for the first edition of the book is Filipino. For the book to reach international readers, I translated it into English. This will be made known to the six continents of the world including Asia, North America, South America, Australia, Europe, and Africa. This will be translated into many various languages so that it can be easily understood by anyone who reads it.

I believe that this millionaire book will be listed on the "**Guinness World Records**" as the best-selling copyright book in the world for having more than 1 billion copies sold. And all these started with only one dream, one book, one small business and one simple Filipino like you who stepped up to become the greatest person to ever live on Earth.

Business expansion will go through after you have managed your business profits efficiently. Learning this will help you achieve your great success in the business world.

MANAGING YOUR BUSINESS PROFIT PERFECTLY

Once your business starts, make sure you know how to compensate the people who work for you. Here is a table of managing your monthly business profits perfectly.

Investor	1%
Founder	4%
Employees' Incentive	5%
Social Responsibility	10%
Chief Executive Officer	10%
Accounting	10%
Marketing	5%
Selling	5%
Purchasing	5%
Quality	10%
Growth	25%
Utilities	10%
Total Profits	**100%**

Compensation for the Investor

You need to compensate 1% of your profits for the investors who were the first people who trusted you and believed that you can manage a business. These are the people who provided for your start-up capital and inspired you to use your God-given genuine talent.

Compensation for the Founder

Compensate 4% of the profits for you as the founder of the business. This will serve as a reward to you who stepped out of establishing your own business. You can use this amount for your family vacations after years of managing your business.

Compensation for Employee Incentive

Reward the people working for the success of your business. Compensate 5% of your profits for those people who have been working competently for your business.

Compensation for Social Responsibility

Consider to compensate 10% of the profits for donations to the church and charity. Giving help to the people who are in need opens the opportunity for more blessings for your business.

Compensation for the CEO

The future of your business lies in the hands of the Chief Executive Officer (CEO). Compensate your CEO by giving 10% of your profits as a gratitude for his or her excellent managerial skills. Managing the company well and working together as a team is the key to your business' success.

Compensation for Accounting

Compensate 10% of your profits for the salary of your accountant who monitors the cash flow of your business. You need a good and trusted Certified Public Accountant to ensure that all your finances are well-managed.

Compensation for Marketing

If you want to have a larger customer base, make sure that you have 5% of your profits for marketing. You need an effective Marketing Executive to ensure that you will have an increasing number of customers that will sustain your business.

Compensation for Selling

If you want to have higher sales of your products or services, the sales team will do that job for you. Compensate 5% of your profits for selling. You need a pleasant-looking Sales Executive that will help get the attention of your target market to ensure that you will have an increasing number of sales that will sustain your business.

Compensation for Purchasing

Compensate 5% of the profits for purchasing the products and services that you need for the continuous operation of your business. You would need a Purchasing Officer who is wise enough to minimize the expenditures of your business capital but can offer you the best possible products that you need.

Compensation for Quality

Have 10% of your profits as funds for improving the quality of your products and services. Improve in quality means more customers will benefit from your business.

Compensation for Growth

Compensate 25% of your profits for the continuous growing operation of your business. This will ensure that you will constantly increase the number of your products and services that you could offer to your customers for the following months.

Compensation for Utilities

The remaining 10% of the profits goes to the usual bills – lease, electricity, water, communications and other fees.

Total Profits

Managing the 100% of your business profits will be a great success if you are able to do so effectively and work together with your team. As your business go through expansion, your profits will also expand as your company offer more products or services to your satisfied clients.

EXAMPLE OF MANAGING YOUR BUSINESS PROFIT PERFECTLY

Let's say I have an initial capital of Php 75,000 in my business for the first month of producing books. The production cost for one book is Php 75, therefore I will be able to produce 1,000 books. Each book will be sold for only Php 300. The computation of the compensation would then be like this.

Name of Funds	Pesos
Initial Capital	75,000
Gross Income	300,000
Business Profit = Gross Income – Initial Capital	225,000
Investor (1%)	2,250
Founder (4%)	9,000
Employees Incentive (5%)	11,250
Social Responsibility (10%)	22,500
Chief Executive Officer (10%)	22,500
Certified Public Accountant (10%)	22,500
Marketing Executive (5%)	11,250
Sales Executive (5%)	11,250
Purchasing Officer (5%)	11,250
Quality Fund (10%)	22,500
Growth Fund (25%)	56,250
Utilities (10%)	22,500

This is just a simple guide that you can use to manage your business profits from producing and selling products on your first month of operation.

BUSINESS PLANNING

A very essential way to succeed in the business world is to have an efficient planning through consistent effort, self-determination and expansion to the entire world.

Business Consistency

An organizational chart system plays a significant role in doing well in your business. This ensures that every process is done consistently and that it will always yield the same result. Having a system in your business enables your employees to work and perform according to their duties and functions. This way, your business automatically runs and be profitable even when you are not physically there.

Business Perseverance

Success does not happen overnight. Perseverance is the key to success. If you are devoted to your business, you will endure with driven purpose and strength at whatever that might come along the way.

Business Expansion

A good entrepreneur plans for expanding his or her business by taking it to the next level. I discovered a way to do this. You can start by doubling your income every month on the first year operation of your business. On the second year, aim to earn the amount you've earned during your entire first year of operations, every month. For the third year, the income for the entire second year must be the target income every month. On the fourth year, your total income from the previous year will be the target income every month. Continue doing this until the fifth year. After 5 years, you would notice that you wouldn't have to work so hard anymore. Your business by this time is already stable and can run on its own.

EXAMPLE OF FIVE YEAR BUSINESS PLANNING

Take a look at this five year business plan of publishing the book entitled *How to Become a Millionaire?* to give you an idea of how to plan for your own business that may help billions of people around the world to become successful and wealthy in all aspects of their lives.

Month	Books Sold (Pieces)	Business Profit (Pesos)	Founder Profit of 4% (Pesos)
December 2014	30	6,750	270
January 2015	60	13,500	540
February 2015	120	27,000	1,080
March 2015	240	54,000	2,160
April 2015	480	108,000	4,320
May 2015	960	216,000	8,640
June 2015	1,920	432,000	17,280
July 2015	3,840	864,000	34,560
August 2015	7,680	1,728,000	69,120
September 2015	15,360	3,456,000	138,240
October 2015	30,720	6,912,000	276,480
November 2015	61,440	13,824,000	552,960
December 2015	122,850	27,641,250	1,105,650
January 2016	122,850	27,641,250	1,105,650
February 2016	122,850	27,641,250	1,105,650
March 2016	122,850	27,641,250	1,105,650

April 2016	122,850	27,641,250	1,105,650
May 2016	122,850	27,641,250	1,105,650
June 2016	122,850	27,641,250	1,105,650
July 2016	122,850	27,641,250	1,105,650
August 2016	122,850	27,641,250	1,105,650
September 2016	122,850	27,641,250	1,105,650
October 2016	122,850	27,641,250	1,105,650
November 2016	122,850	27,641,250	1,105,650
December 2016	1,474,200	331,695,000	13,267,800
January 2017	1,474,200	331,695,000	13,267,800
February 2017	1,474,200	331,695,000	13,267,800
March 2017	1,474,200	331,695,000	13,267,800
April 2017	1,474,200	331,695,000	13,267,800
May 2017	1,474,200	331,695,000	13,267,800
June 2017	1,474,200	331,695,000	13,267,800
July 2017	1,474,200	331,695,000	13,267,800
August 2017	1,474,200	331,695,000	13,267,800
September 2017	1,474,200	331,695,000	13,267,800
October 2017	1,474,200	331,695,000	13,267,800
November 2017	1,474,200	331,695,000	13,267,800
December 2017	17,690,400	3,980,340,000	159,213,600
January 2018	17,690,400	3,980,340,000	159,213,600
February 2018	17,690,400	3,980,340,000	159,213,600
March 2018	17,690,400	3,980,340,000	159,213,600
April 2018	17,690,400	3,980,340,000	159,213,600
May 2018	17,690,400	3,980,340,000	159,213,600
June 2018	17,690,400	3,980,340,000	159,213,600
July 2018	17,690,400	3,980,340,000	159,213,600
August 2018	17,690,400	3,980,340,000	159,213,600
September 2018	17,690,400	3,980,340,000	159,213,600
October 2018	17,690,400	3,980,340,000	159,213,600
November 2018	17,690,400	3,980,340,000	159,213,600
December 2019	212,284,800	47,764,080,000	1,910,563,200
January 2019	212,284,800	47,764,080,000	1,910,563,200
February 2019	212,284,800	47,764,080,000	1,910,563,200
March 2019	212,284,800	47,764,080,000	1,910,563,200
April 2019	212,284,800	47,764,080,000	1,910,563,200
May 2019	212,284,800	47,764,080,000	1,910,563,200
June 2019	212,284,800	47,764,080,000	1,910,563,200
July 2019	212,284,800	47,764,080,000	1,910,563,200
August 2019	212,284,800	47,764,080,000	1,910,563,200
September 2019	212,284,800	47,764,080,000	1,910,563,200
October 2019	212,284,800	47,764,080,000	1,910,563,200
November 2019	212,284,800	47,764,080,000	1,910,563,200
Financial Statement by December 2019	**2,778,989,850**	**625,272,716,250**	**25,010,908,650**

In this example, I am able to generate profits by producing the millionaire book as a creative product of my God-given genuine talent. I started selling with one book and I am now able to sell almost 3 billion copies all over the world.

Compensating the 4% of the business profits to the founder of the business, this amount would be equivalent to more than 25 billion pesos! This amount is enough for millions of happy family vacations and living in financial freedom. If you will be using the five-year plan for your business expansion, you will definitely become successful and wealthy in just 5 years of working smart in your own business.

After you have completed the seventh step of opening your millionaire's business, your eighth step will be...

INSPIRATIONAL QUOTES ABOUT BUSINESS

"I find out what the world needs.
Then I go ahead and try to invent it"
— THOMAS EDISON, Creator of *First Incandescent Bulb*

"The success of every entrepreneur relies on a
happy family and home."
— JOEY CONCEPCION, Founder of *Go Negosyo*

"I believe that tourism is the way to go for the Philippines to
survive in global competitiveness.
The Filipinos are a breed of fun-loving, hospitable, and
service-oriented people. The ingredients of becoming a
world-class destination are already here."
-BEN CHAN, Founder of *Bench*

"The traditional role of business is to provide goods and
services for a profit. Businesses have to make money, because
if they don't, it's not sustainable."
-MANNY PANGILINAN, Founder of *Metro Pacific Investment Corp.*

"My entrepreneurial career has been a roller coaster ride,
with so many loops and hurdles along the way. But I know
that you can win all the challenges if you are armed with
sheer determination, clear intensions, and self-discipline."
-EDGAR SIA II, Founder of *Mang Inasal*

"What this power is, I cannot say; all I know is that it exists
and it becomes available only when a man is in that state of
mind in which he knows exactly what he wants and is fully
determined not to quit until he finds it."
— ALEXANDER GRAHAM BELL, Creator of *First Telephone*

"Wealth is within everybody's reach. All it takes is to have the
proper discipline, determination, and decisiveness to be
financially savvy."
-FRANCISCO COLAYCO, Author of *Wealth Within Your Reach*

THE MILLIONAIRE'S BUSINESS

"The creative business is the process of producing new product or service that helps millions of people around the world."
-ENGR. RICH MAGPANTAY

The seventh step of becoming a millionaire is by opening your millionaire's business. Your business must be creative in order to produce new innovative products or services that help millions of people. Open your start-up business with this eight simple process: know your genuine talent, discover how you can help others; create a good business name; have your business registered with the proper authorities; produce your creative products or services; sell your products or services; improve the quality of the product or service you are offering; and expand your business. Perform ideal financial management of your business profits by compensating 1% for the investors, 4% for the founders, 5% for employee incentives, 10% for business administration, 10% for accounting, 5% for marketing, 5% for selling, 5% for purchasing, 10% for quality, 25% for growth, and 10% for utilities. Make a five year business planning for your expansion to the entire world.

SEVENTH MILLIONAIRE TRAINING

I. The Millionaire Business

1. How many days would it take for your one peso investment to become 100 million pesos if you will double the earning every single day?

2. What will be your innovative product for your start-up business using your genuine talent?

3. What will be your professional service that you can offer?

4. Why are Filipino-Chinese engaged in business?

5. Should you be consistent to continue your business to become successful?

6. Will you persevere to lead your business to success and make it known to the entire world?

7. Is it your dream to work smart for only 5 years using your genuine talent in establishing your own business?

8. Is it your dream to work smart for only 5 years and then spend the rest of your life with family going on happy vacations and living in financial freedom?

II. Opening a start-up business.

1. What is your genuine talent?

2. What is your creative concept for your products and services to help people?

3. What is a good name for your business?

4. When should you go to DTI to register your business?

5. When will you start creating your products or services?

6. When will you start selling your products or services to the market?

7. When will you start working seriously for your business to improve its quality?

8. Is it your dream to take your products and services to the entire world?

III. If you have a business that enables you to earn a profit of 1,000,000 pesos every month, how much will be the compensation for:

Investor (1%)	Php
Founder (4%)	Php
Employee Incentives (5%)	Php
Social Responsibility (10%)	Php
CEO (10%)	Php
Accountant (10%)	Php
Marketing (5%)	Php
Selling (5%)	Php
Purchasing (5%)	Php
Quality (10%)	Php
Growth (25%)	Php
Utilities (10%)	Php

STEP 8
THE MILLIONAIRE'S HABIT

"Successful men become successful only because they acquire the habit of thinking in terms of success."
—NAPOLEON HILL, Author of *Law of Success*

HABIT
Pattern: A person's behavior or movement that he or she does repeatedly as part of his or her beliefs.
-Definition by ENGR. RICH MAGPANTAY

THE POWERFUL HABIT

The powerful habit that I will explain to you is based on my personal experience and from those of successful and wealthy people such as Napoleon Hill, Robert Kiyosaki and John Calub.

Because of Napoleon Hill, I dreamed of becoming an internationally famous author by writing a best-selling millionaire book. Because of Robert Kiyosaki, I learned to find ways to become truly wealthy. Because of John Calub, I learned to do attractive activities to achieve genuine success in my life. Because of the people who inspired me, I found the master key to success and wealth through the concept of this powerful habit, which will open the greatest opportunity for you to become successful and wealthy in all aspects of your life: emotional, intellectual, spiritual, physical, and financial.

STORY OF THE NUMBER 28

In my life's journey, I discovered how powerful the number 28 is in achieving my precise dreams. I passed the licensure examination for Electronics Engineering after 28 days of intensive self-studying. I wrote the book *How to Become a Millionaire?* for 28 weeks. After 28 months of romantic relationship, my wife and I got married on the 28th day of December. After 28 years of life existence, my dream of having my own house and car came true. I learned that one peso can turn into 100 million pesos in just 28 days by compounding interest every day. According to the Law of Seven, what I have learned can become a part of my belief system after 28 days. Because of these experiences, I am certain that there is power in the number 28 which I can use to turn my precise dreams into reality. Therefore, I can use the number 28 as my basis for forming the powerful habits of becoming genuinely successful and truly wealthy.

THE GRAND MISSION

The grand mission of a person like you in this world is to learn how you can become the greatest contributor to the economy of mankind. This grand mission will determine the activities that you will do in order to help others and achieve the success that you desire. The grand mission will also develop your character to be the person you want to become.

In my experience, I worked enthusiastically on my grand mission of being an internationally famous author by writing the concepts every single day until I completed the book. I also thought of various ways to do research about the contents of the topic to be discussed in the book with the help of the people I have met. I wrote this book while I was on board the ship. After working for 8 hours, I used my spare time in writing the book. I got the ideas from the experiences I had with my colleagues on the ship, all the wonderful events I had while I was travelling the six continents of the world, my personal experiences, the books I have read about success and wealth, stories of famous people and loved ones, inspirational movies, romantic music, and the steps I take for every opportunity I have. I believe that all the genuine success and true wealth that I have today starts with a single step by knowing my grand mission.

CREATOR OF THE WORLD'S POWERFUL MILLIONAIRE PRAYER

I believe that the life purpose of every person in the world is to serve others by using our own genuine talent to produce a new creative product or service that can bring satisfaction and convenience to people in the entire world. I also learned that in just five years of running a creative business, you can achieve massive wealth by helping millions of people. Because of this principle, I am able to create a prayer that you can use to achieve prosperity and abundance so that it can help you become successful and wealthy in all aspect of your life: emotional, intellectual, spiritual, physical, and financial. The brand name is called "**The Millionaire Prayer**" which I believe is now becoming "**World's Powerful Millionaire Prayer**" for achieving genuine success and true wealth.

THE MILLIONAIRE PRAYER

The Millionaire Prayer is composed of eight statements that must be declared for 28 consecutive days. It must be declared once you wake up in the morning and declared again before you go to sleep at night. Declare the prayer with your eyes open, and declare it again with your eyes closed. Do this while feeling great, enthusiastic and energized within 28 minutes.

This prayer will help you to achieve success and wealth by being optimistic in life. By having a positive thinking, this prayer will be the master key to achieve happiness in all aspects of your life. Declaring this prayer will help you to condition your mind and develop self-confidence every day and every night.

EIGHT STATEMENTS OF
THE MILLIONAIREPRAYER

These are the eight statements of the millionaire prayer:
1. The success that you want to achieve.
2. The activities that you love to do.
3. The activities you would do to serve the world.
4. The wealth that you want to have.
5. The wealth that you need to share.
6. The good health and love for family.
7. The love for other people and nature.
8. Thanksgiving to God.

The First Statement

The first sentence states the success you want to achieve in life. Your success is based on your God-given genuine talent, which you can use to serve millions of people.

The Second Statement

The second sentence states the activities that you love doing using your God-given genuine talent.

The Third Statement

The third sentence states the reason why you want to serve the world using your God-given genuine talent.

The Fourth Statement

The fourth sentence states the wealth that you want to achieve within five years. This wealth can be based on the date of your birth.

The Fifth Statement

The fifth sentence states the wealth that you need to share from your income to help the needy people, the church and charity. The wealth that you receive is more meaningful if you will use this to help others according to the Law of Giving—giving tithes equivalent to 10% of your income.

The Sixth Statement

The sixth sentence states your desire to have good health and love for your family. Having a good physical health is of great importance for achieving wealth.

The Seventh Statement

The seventh sentence states that you are living happy, loving and grateful for other people and the nature around you.

The Eighth Statement

The eighth sentence states the thanksgiving to God for the success and wealth you are achieving in your life's journey. Giving thanks to God in every moment of your life is the master key to your prosperity and abundance in the world.

EXAMPLE OF THE MILLIONAIRE PRAYER

I believe it is my grand mission to serve people through writing the book, *How to Become a Millionaire?*, to help anyone who read it of becoming successful and wealthy in all aspects of his or her life. By using my genuine talent of being intelligent, optimistic in life and being passionate on books, I am able inspire more than 1 billion people. The success I desire is to become an internationally famous author. I was truly loved when I wrote the book because I know that I can produce more than 1 billion copies of the book in the entire world and it will be written in various languages. The wealth that I want to earn five years from now (on January 13, 2019) is 13 billion pesos. I will declare the prayer while feeling great, enthusiastic and energized. I wrote my Millionaire Prayer in a piece of paper and put my name, date and commit my signature on it.

Here's the Millionaire Prayer I made as an example.

1. "I feel great, enthusiastic and energized today that I am becoming the greatest best-selling millionaire book author in the world."

2. "I feel great, enthusiastic and energized today that I am loving to write the book *How to Become a Millionaire?* and it is being sold worldwide for more than 1 billion copies in various languages."

3. "I feel great, enthusiastic and energized today that I am serving more than 1 billion people around the world and teaching them of becoming successful and wealthy in all aspects of their lives: emotional, intellectual, spiritual, physical, and financial while they are reading the book I wrote."

4. "I feel great, enthusiastic and energized today that I am earning 13 billion pesos or more better by January 13, 2019."

5. "I feel great, enthusiastic and energized today that I am giving 1.3 billion pesos to the needy people, the church and charity."

6. "I feel great, enthusiastic and energized today that I am having a perfectly healthy body and becoming the greatest loving husband, father, son and friend."

7. "I feel great, enthusiastic and energized today that I am living a happy, loving and grateful life with all the great people I know and with the beautiful nature surrounding me."

8. "Thank you so much, God, for this wonderful journey of success and wealth, and today is the greatest day I ever have in my life."

DECLARING THE MILLIONAIRE PRAYER

Declaring the Millionaire Prayer requires a powerful emotion of feeling great, enthusiastic and energized. You have to believe that everything you affirm in prayer is happening to you right now. This might come as a challenge because your thinking will positively transform you in the next 28 days while declaring the prayer. You have to be consistent in the way you declare the prayer for 28 consecutive days. You have to declare it with confidence for 28 days, two times a day: in the morning upon waking up and at night before you sleep. You also have to declare the prayer twice each time: while reading it aloud and then memorizing it with eyes closed, declaring it with an intense emotion. In this way, your belief will have a positive effect on success and wealth, and that every good thing that you dream of will eventually come your way. All you need to do is become self-disciplined in committing on every declaration that you have made in the Millionaire Prayer.

YOUR 28 DAYS' ACTIVITIES OF SUCCESS AND WEALTH

The activities written here are your guide of conditioning your mind to prosperity and abundance in 28 consecutive days. What is important here is to develop your self-discipline on performing all the activities even when no one is watching you. Through these 28 consecutive days of activities, your belief will certainly positively transform into the desired success and wealth you have dreamed of.

Day 1: Create and Declare Your Own Millionaire Prayer

Creating your own millionaire prayer will help to know the direction of your life every single day as you take on your journey towards success and wealth. All you have to do is create the eight sentences stating: your success; activity that you love to do; activity that you will do to serve others; desired wealth; sharing your wealth; loving yourself and family; loving others and nature; and being grateful to God. Write your millionaire prayer on a piece of paper together with your name, date and signature. And post it on the wall where you can easily see it when you wake up and before going to sleep.

After you have created your own millionaire prayer, declare your prayer when you wake in the morning twice - while reading it aloud and with closed eyes - within 28 minutes for 28 consecutive days. Then before you go to sleep in the evening, declare your prayer again twice. While declaring the prayer, you have to feel great, enthusiastic and energized for you to believe what you are praying for.

Day 2: Write Your Grand Mission on Your Business Card

Write your grand mission at the back of your business card so that it will remind you of the things you need to do to achieve success in your life. The grand mission is the first statement of your Millionaire Prayer.

Day 3: Write Your Grand Mission on Your Drinking Water Glass

Write your grand mission on your drinking water glass. I believe that water has its own memory. If you declare your grand mission over water, your mission will be transferred in the memory of water. When you drink this water with the memory of your grand mission, it will go through your body system and absorb the emotions you have. When this water leaves your body and starts travelling into different places on Earth, this will bring the people you need for the fulfillment of your grand mission.

Source: Masaru Emoto's Water Theory

Day 4: Create Your Millionaire's Check

Write the amount of 1 million pesos on a blank check, indicating your name, signature and the date today, and place it in your wallet. This will remind you that you are earning 1 million pesos income every month because of this principle.

Day 5: Create Your Millionaire's Cash

Write the amount of 1 million pesos on a sheet of paper and place it in your wallet. This way, you will be reminded of the wealth that you have in your wallet.

Day 6: GREAT Greetings

Learn to greet everyone by saying "**GREAT morning!**" no matter what time of the day it is. When you greet someone, it helps you to become more productive because it makes you think of a brand new day and the people you greet. The simple meaning for GREAT is:

G-ratitude
R-espect
E-njoy
A-dmire
T-alent

Gratitude for someone brings happiness; *Respect* for someone knows uniqueness, *Enjoy* the day by showing your smile to others, *Admire* someone for his or her strength and *Talent* day remind others to do what they love to do.

Day 7: Admiring Words

You have to say admiring words and compliment to your loved ones, colleagues, friends and acquaintances every time you talk to them. Whenever you do this, you are helping other people to feel good about themselves because of the compliments that you tell them. You will be remembered by the people through your appreciative words. Admire them by saying, "**Be the GREATEST person to ever live!**"

The meaning of GREATEST is:
G-rateful
R-espectful
E-njoyable
A-dmirable
T-alented
E-nthusiastic
S-ervice-oriented
T-oday

Being a *Grateful* person has a character to say thank you every time you receive something. Being *Respectful* is to accept unique character of every person. *Enjoyable* person is a positive thinker. *Admirable* simply appreciates the good things of others. To do what you love is a *Talented* person. To be able to show your good work while full of energy means *Enthusiastic*. Always be in *Service* to others. Live at a present moment *Today*. Remember that only today is the greatest day you will ever have in your life.

Day 8: The Magic of Singing

Whenever you sing songs that touch the heart, your genuine talent is awakened and you feel inspired. You can also feel the positive energy flowing through your body every time you sing.

Day 9: Listening to Inspirational Music

Listening to instrumentals songs or sounds of nature will also give you inspiration and ability to receive great ideas from the universe while you are in the reflection process.

Day 10: Writing Your Gratitude

You will discover that writing is a good way to manifest your gratitude to God every day, which also serves as a channel for precise dreams to come true. Wealthy and successful people are always grateful for what they have. On your notebook, recall the good things that had happened to you during the entire day, and write at least eight reasons why you should be thankful. Write also your advanced thanksgiving for the success and wealth that you desire in all aspects of your life.

Day 11: Reading Success Books

Reading books and biographies written by successful and wealthy people every day is an important habit because it will give you a strong sense of inspiration and desire to achieve your precise dreams. Reading will also help you develop the right habits for success and wealth. It will also give you proper guidance in creating a positive outlook for your journey towards wealth and success. When reading, it is best to listen to instrumental music or to the sounds of nature.

Day 12: Giving Help

Reaching out to charity, church and those in need is a good habit if you want to have a true wealth. Giving 10% of your income to people who need financial help like relatives, those who are living in the streets, to the church and charity is the true essence of having wealth in the world. Wealth becomes meaningful when you use it to help someone in need. By being generous, you will receive more blessings in return in various forms such as good health, job promotion, or increasing number of customers and sales for the business. This habit is based on the Law of Giving.

Day 13: Dinning in a Fine Restaurant

Try dinning out at a superb restaurant. Dinning out gives you a sense of confidence that you are wealthy because you can have a meal at any restaurant you want. It will also give you the feeling that it would be easy to get rich and to achieve what you want. After all, if the rich can eat at such fine restaurants, then you can also.

Day 14: Creating Your SMART Dream Board

Creating a "**SMART dream**" board that you can always see reminds you that you have a desired success and wealth that you want to achieve. Make a collection of your dreams by cutting out pictures of your dreams. Place these pictures on a green cardboard and post it on the wall where you can always see it.

Having a SMART dream meaning:
S-ee
M-easure
A-mount
R-eal
T-ime

It is essential that you must be able to *See* the picture of your dreams. Your dreams should also be *Measureable*, meaning it is precise and tangible. The *Amount* of your success should also be precise. Your dream should also be *Realistic,* meaning you know how to achieve your dreams. You should also have a *Time* frame when you want to achieve you dream. That is the SMART way to do on your precise dream. Your SMART dream will give you the direction you need so that you will always be inspired to continue your written goals and strive until it turns into success. It is very important to have your precise dream so that it will surely come true. It must be in all aspects of your life: emotional love for God, your family, nature and your country, intellectual capability with your success mentor, spiritual state in total communion with your holy church, physical health of your body and financial wealth you desire.

Day 15: Taking Pictures with Your Loving Family While Holding this Millionaire Book

From experience, I've seen how taking photographs of the precise green dreams could give a new sense of motivation to achieve these dreams. Together with your loved ones, start taking pictures of you SMART dreams like car, home, business, things and activities that you want to have in your life. Be precise in terms of the model home you want to live in, the brand of the car that you want to drive, business type you want to manage, fashionable things you want to have and adventure activities you want to do.

Once you have those pictures of your SMART dreams, always look at them every single day. The Law of Attraction will find a way for these things to come to you because what you think will positively happen.

Day 16: Taking Pictures with Your Success Mentor

Day 17: Taking Pictures with a View of Your Holy Church

Day 18: Taking Pictures of Your Perfectly Healthy Body

Day 19: Taking Pictures of Your Desired Wealth

**Day 20: Taking Pictures with
Your SMART Dream Car**

**Day 21: Taking Pictures with
Your SMART Dream Home**

**Day 22: Taking Pictures with
Your SMART Dream Business**

**Day 23: Taking Pictures with
Your SMART Dream Things**

**Day 24: Taking Pictures with
Your SMART Dream Activities**

Day 25: Developing Your Creative Genius

I have developed my creative genius because of these experiences: I have great inspiration, I am so in love, I dream of being famous, I learned how to sing, I make friends, I cooperate with others, I have been through a lot in my life, and I pray every single day. I know I need all of these so that I can develop my creative genius as I write this millionaire book. I was truly inspired by the lives of successful and wealthy people even before I wrote this book. I also have this passionate love for my wife, children and God. I knew that it was my grand mission to become a best-selling author of books on success and wealth. While working on the book, I listened to good music such as instrumentals and sound of nature. I had friends and colleagues who helped me out in completing the book because of their stories and advice. I knew that my life purpose is to help or serve all the people I meet so they can also find happiness. I remembered the times when my wife could not afford what she wants because we were not earning enough that time. I believe that the Millionaire Prayer I wrote will help many people to make their dreams come true. All of these were essential for me to develop my creative genius.

I want to let you experience all of these feeling in order for you to become a creative genius.

Day 26: Continuing Your Grand Mission

Working every day for your grand mission in life is the effective step towards genuine success and true wealth using your God-given genuine talent. Make every day as a brand new day to focus on the completion of your grand mission.

Day 27: Strengthening Your Grand Mission

Strengthening to expand your grand mission is the master key for you to achieve genuine success and true wealth in the world. This grand mission should always aim to help millions of people. By declaring your Millionaire Prayer every day and by visualizing at your SMART dreams, you will be able to attract the people who can help you to improve and expand your grand mission. You can associate with people with the same vision together so you can create unique products or services that can be shared to the entire world.

Day 28: Forming Your Creative Alliance

Making friends and investing in good relationships with people who have the same vision as yours will help you to create your own alliance. This group will be able to create the unique products and services you need through the collective efforts of the members. In this group, each member will contribute to the success of the business as each one takes a significant role in the business: one for operational management, one for finances and resources, one for marketing and distribution, and one for purchasing and acquisition. This way, the success of the business does not only rely on one person. All members of the group will be working together towards their success.

After you have completed the eighth step of taking action of your millionaire's habit, you're now in a journey towards...

INSPIRATIONAL QUOTES ABOUT HABIT

*"The thing I really care about is mission,
making the world open."*
– MARK ZUCKERBERG, Founder of *Facebook*

"Focus on your future. Your greatness is waiting for you."
— BO SANCHEZ, Founder of *Light of Jesus* Community

*"I want to help you achieve your dreams and
make you multi-millionaire!"*
—JOHN CALUB, *Philippines No.1 Success Coach*

"Carry your most important goal in your wallet."
— JACK CANFIELD, Author of *The Success Principles*

*"Choose a job you love, and you will never have
to work a day in your life."*
— CONFUCIUS, Author of *The Great Learning*

*"The most important thing in life is to learn
how to give out love, and to let it come in."*
— MITCH ALBOM, Author of *Tuesdays with Morrie*

*"Our beliefs about what we are and what we can be,
precisely determine what we will be."*
— ANTHONY ROBBINS, Author of *Awaken the Giant Within*

"Every morning we are born again.
What we do today is what matters most."
— GAUTAMA BUDDHA, Author of *The Sayings of the Buddha*

*"You have the power to change your future by making an
important decision today. Let go of the past!"*
— CHINKEE TAN, Author of *Till Debt Do Us Part*

*"You are today where your thoughts have brought you;
you will be tomorrow where your thoughts take you."*
- JAMES ALLEN, Author of *As a Man Thinketh*

THE MILLIONAIRE'S HABIT

"The powerful habit will transform your believe leading to your genuine success."
-ENGR. RICH MAGPANTAY

The eighth step of becoming a millionaire is taking action on your millionaire's habit. These habits are: creating your own Millionaire Prayer and declaring it for 28 consecutive days; writing your grand mission on your business card and on your drinking glass, having a 1 million peso check and cash; greeting everyone with GREAT morning, admiring words, singing and listening to inspiring music, writing gratitude, giving help, reading books, dining in a fine restaurants, having SMART dream board, taking pictures of these universal dreams, continuing and strengthening your grand mission, and forming your creative alliance. Doing all these habits will transform you of becoming successful and wealthy in all aspects of your life: emotional, intellectual, spiritual, physical, and financial.

EIGHTH MILLIONAIRE TRAINING

I. Write your own Millionaire Prayer:
1. What is your first statement in the prayer?

2. What is your second statement in the prayer?

3. What is your third statement in the prayer?

4. What is your fourth statement in the prayer?

5. What is your fifth statement in the prayer?

6. What is your sixth statement in the prayer?

7. What is your seventh statement in the prayer?

8. What is your eighth statement in the prayer?

II. For 28 days, self-discipline to do the following:

1. A. Declaring your Millionaire Prayer for 28 consecutive days when you wake up in the morning, twice: while reading it out loud, and with your eyes closed, with great feeling.

   B. Declaring your Millionaire Prayer for 28 consecutive days before you go to sleep at night, twice: while reading it out loud, and with your eyes closed, with great feeling.

2. Writing your grand mission on your business card.

3. Writing your grand mission on your drinking glass.

4. Writing the amount of 1 million pesos on a blank check and put it inside your wallet.

5. Writing the amount of 1 million pesos on paper and put it inside your wallet.

6. Greeting everyone with "GREAT Morning".

7. Giving admiring words to everyone.

8. Expressing your gratitude by writing up the things that happens in a day and the success you desire.

9. Singing inspirational songs that touch your heart.

10. Listening to instrumental music and sounds of nature

11. Reading books written by successful and wealthy people.

12. Giving help to those people in need, tithes to church and donations to charity.

13. Dining in a fine restaurant.

14. Making collections for your SMART dreams board.

15. Taking pictures with your loving family while holding this millionaire book.

16. Taking pictures with your success mentor.

17. Taking pictures with a view of your holy church.

18. Taking pictures of your healthy body.

19. Taking pictures of your desire wealth.

20. Taking pictures with your SMART dream car.

21. Taking pictures with your SMART dream home.

22. Taking pictures with your SMART dream business.

23. Taking pictures with your SMART dream things.

24. Taking pictures with your SMART dream activities.

25. Developing your creative genius.

26. Continuing your grand mission.

27. Strengthening your grand mission.

28. Forming your creative alliance.

JOURNEY
BECOMING A MILLIONAIRE NOW

"The journey of a thousand miles begins with a single step."
-CHINESE PROVERB

PRAYER
Faith: a spiritual belief in God.
-Definition by ENGR. RICH MAGPANTAY

THE CONSISTENT PRAYING

Praying is the most important activity of all the effective steps that are written on this book of becoming successful and wealthy in all aspects of your life. Through consistent prayers, you will develop the faith that will make you believe that you can have everything you've always dreamed of while declaring your millionaire prayer with a great feeling. Having this faith will give you the inspiration you need to achieve all your heart's desires because you will find that everything can be done and that everything is possible. This way, you will be able to do small steps towards your success in achieving your grand mission to serve millions of people around the world.

JOURNEY OF BECOMING A MILLIONAIRE

Your journey towards your genuine success and true wealth using the eight effective steps of becoming a millionaire begins with the first step, which is by having a positive outlook in life towards your genuine talent. It is also important that you write your precise dreams, which is the second step of becoming a millionaire. The third step is about following the universal laws of prosperity and abundance. Of course, wealth will only be meaningful if this will be used to help other people, which is the fourth step of becoming a millionaire. The fifth step is about the perfect financial handling of your income. The sixth step is about investing in various businesses to increase your wisdom, while the seventh step of becoming a millionaire is about starting your own business using your genuine talent. The eighth step is taking action for 28 consecutive days to condition your mind to transform you to become successful and wealthy in all aspects of your life: emotional, intellectual, spiritual, physical, and financial.

TAKING SMALL STEPS TOWARDS SUCCESS

Doing small steps towards your genuine success is very significant to achieve your dreams. All great things start from humble beginnings. For every small step you make, you are one step closer to your desired success. Being happy, loving and grateful millionaire in all aspects of your life begins now through the knowledge you have learned from this millionaire book; apply it every day to achieve the prosperity and abundance. To become genuinely successful, transform to have a positive attitude in life, take every possible step towards your written goal, and continue to work for your grand mission until you reach the success and wealth you desire. Remember that today is the greatest day you will ever have in your life.

BECOMING A MILLIONAIRE NOW

Making your decision now is essential as you begin your journey towards the realization of your dream of becoming successful and wealthy in all aspects of your life. You have already made a good decision now to do every step written in this book for you to achieve your precise dreams faster by using your genuine talent. Make a commitment now that you are declaring every day and every night your millionaire prayer.

THE WORLD'S SUCCESSFUL AND WEALTHY PEOPLE

The lives of the successful and wealthy people inspired me to write this book. I believe they continue to take small possible steps every moment of every day for their dream success to come true.

Just like Thomas Edison who invented the incandescent bulb that brought the light to every home; Brothers Wilbur and Orville Wright who invented the airplane that brought people to distant places by air; Alexander Graham Bell who invented the telephone that connected people wherever they are; Henry Ford who invented the car that brought people to various places by land; Bill Gates who founded *Microsoft* that made every business transaction faster; Dr. Jose Rizal who wrote *Noli Me Tangere* and *El*

Filibusterismo that revived nationalism among Filipinos; Socorro Ramos who founded *National Bookstore* that provided books to more Filipinos; Henry Sy who founded the *SM Malls* that provided millions of jobs to Filipinos; Edgar Sia of *Mang Inasal* who served the best-tasting grilled chicken in the country; Bo Sanchez who founded *The Light of Jesus* Community to spread the Good News of God; Napoleon Hill who wrote *Think and Grow Rich* that helped people achieve their precise dreams; Robert Kiyosaki who wrote *Rich Dad Poor Dad* that taught people the truth about wealth; John Calub who taught people the easy way to success; and Engr. Rich Magpantay who wrote *How to Become a Millionaire?* to share the wisdom in achieving the precise dream, genuine success and true wealth that most people desire.

THE TWO VERSES OF TRUTH

There are two Biblical verses that support the truth of the ideas written on this book.

Genesis 1:26 states, "*Let us make mankind in our image, in our likeness, so that they may rule over the fish in the sea and the birds in the sky, over the livestock and all the wild animals, and over all the creatures that move along the ground.*" This verse means that you have the power to control anything by using your personal genuine talent.

Matthew 21:22 states, "*If you believe, you will receive whatever you ask for in prayer.*" In everything you do, you will receive whatever you ask through prayer. This only means that all your precise dreams will come true if you pray for it and believe it with all of your heart.

LET YOUR SMART DREAMS COME

Let your SMART dreams come into your way by taking responsible action on the eight effective steps of becoming successful and wealthy in all aspects of your life: emotional, intellectual, spiritual, physical, and financial. Use your God-given genuine talent to serve more people for you to achieve the genuine success and true wealth in the world. You have the power to intensify your genuine talent and to do everything according to your own desire to achieve prosperity and abundance. You have to serve millions of people on Earth which is the reason for your life existence.

Be the GREATEST person to ever live,

ENGR. RICH MAGPANTAY

YOUR MILLIONAIRE JOURNEY

*"Whatever SMART dreams that you desire,
as long as you're praying for it,
believing it in your heart and
using your genuine talent in taking action,
it will surely coming your way."*
-ENGR. RICH MAGPANTAY, Author of
How to Become a Millionaire?

GRATEFUL REQUEST

*Please **SHARE** this Millionaire Book to at least two (2) persons you LOVE and CARE about.*

*If this Millionaire Book you read is of GREAT value for you and helps you to achieve your SMART dream, please DONATE with LOVE One Philippine Peso **(PHP 1)** or One American Dollar **(USD 1)** in order for us to continue helping billions of people around the world to live in a better and happier life.*

*Please send your **LOVE DONATION** to:*

Peso Account
Bank/Branch: Bank of Philippine Islands / Santa Rosa
Account Name: Arjay Magpantay
Account Number: 8519-3833-07

Or

Dollar Account
Bank/Branch: Philippine National Bank / Santa Rosa
Account Name: Arjay Magpantay
Account Number: 4923-1390-0015

Thank you, thank you, thank you for being generous.

Be the GREATEST person to ever live on Earth.

GOD wants you to be happy!

SUCCESS QUOTE

"It took multiple refusals from several publishers before J.K. Rowling to produce the best-selling novel, HARRY POTTER.

It took 242 attempts before Howard Schultz was finally able to make the best-selling coffee and put up his own coffee shop named STARBUCKS.

It took 302 efforts before Walt Disney was able to perfect his theme park concept, DISNEYLAND.

It took 1,009 tries before Colonel Sanders was able to sell the unbeatable chicken recipe at KENTUCKY FRIED CHICKEN.

It took 1,500 shots before Sylvester Stallone able to use the script he wrote and start filming his movie, ROCKY.

Always remember this:

It takes consistent action for you to succeed.

Keep going and believe you can do it."

-RICHMIND

RICHMIND INVESTMENT GUIDE

SUCCESS BOOKS
- *Think and Grow Rich* by Napoleon Hill
- *The Master-Key to Riches* by Napoleon Hill
- *Law of Success* by Napoleon Hill
- *Rich Dad, Poor Dad* by Robert Kiyosaki with Sharon Lecter
- *Rich Dad's Cashflow Quadrant* by Robert Kiyosaki
- *Rich Dad's Retire Rich Retire Young* by Robert Kiyosaki
- *How to Become a Millionaire?* by Engr. Rich Magpantay
- *Paano Maging Milyonaryo?* by Engr. Rich Magpantay
- *8 Secrets of the Truly Rich* by Bo Sanchez
- *8 Habits of the Happy Millionaire* by Bo Sanchez
- *How to Do the Impossible* by Bo Sanchez
- *Stop Hidden Addictions* by Bo Sanchez
- *My Maid Invest in the Stock Market* by Bo Sanchez
- *The Master Key System* by Charles Haanel
- *The Science of Getting Rich* by Wallace Wattles
- *The Success Principles* by Jack Canfield with Janet Switzer
- *The 100 Absolutely Unbreakable Laws of Business Success* by Brian Tracy
- *Maximum Achievement* by Brian Tracy
- *The Millionaire Next Door* by Dr. Thomas Stanley & Dr. Danko
- *Secrets of the Millionaire Mind* of T. Harv Eker
- *10 Secrets for Success and Inner* Peace by Dr. Wayne Dyer
- *Who Moved My Cheese?* by Dr. Spencer Johnson
- *Awaken the Giant Within* by Anthony Robbins
- *Winning with People* by John Maxwell
- *My Philosophy for Successful Living* by Jim Rohn
- *The 7 Habits of Highly Effective People* by Stephen Covey
- *You Were Born Rich* by Bob Proctor
- *The Secret* by Rhonda Byrne
- *The Magic* by Rhonda Byrne
- *The E-Myth Revisited* by Michael Gerber
- *Born to Win* by Zig Ziglar
- *The One Minute Manager* by Kenneth Blanchard
- *The Time Keeper* by Mitch Albom
- *As a Man Thinketh* by James Allen
- *Outliers* by Malcolm Gladwell
- *The Power of Positive Thinking* by Norman Vincent Peale
- *How to Win Friends and Influence People* by Dale Carnegie

- *The Most Important Minute* by Ken Dunn
- *The Success System That Never Fails* by W. Clement Stone
- *The Essays of Warren Buffet* by Warren Buffet
- *The Joy in Loving* by Mother Teresa
- *The Holy Bible*
- *The Great Learning* by Confucious
- *The Sayings of Buddha*
- *The Holy Qur'an*
- *Go Negosyo 55 Inspiring Stories of Women Entrepreneurs* by Joey Concepcion
- *Investing in the Stock Market Today* by COL Financial Inc
- *8 Simple Tips for Young Entrepreneurs* by John Rodica
- *Glimpse to Enlightenment* by Sherwin Sobrepena
- *Pinoy MLM Expose* by Eduard Reformina
- *Money and Me* by Sha Nacino
- *I Ordered My Future Yesterday* by Julie Cox
- *Till Debt Do Us Part* by Chinkee Tan
- *Think Rich Pinoy* by Larry Gamboa
- *Wealth Within Your Reach* by Francisco Colayco
- *Negosyong Patok* by Ma. Aurora Sicat
- *Paano Mapasasaya si Misis?* By Dr. William Orr

FINANCIAL TRAININGS

- *How to Become a Millionaire* by Engr. Rich Magpantay
- *How to Make Millions in the Stock Market* by Bo Sanchez
- *How to Make Your Passion Your Profession* by Sha Nacino
- *How to Be a Best Selling Author* by Jay Mclean
- *How to Become a Money Magnet* by John Calub
- *How to Unleash the Power Within* of Team Pinoy Wave
- *Train the Trainors* of G-Cell Support System
- *Universal Success Boot Camp* by Gelyn Valenzuela
- *Stock Market Technical Analysis* of COL Financial Inc
- *Comprehensive Approach in Real Estate Selling* of Driven Marketing Group, Inc
- *Financial Literacy* of Seafarers Entrustment Association
- *Training Course for Instructors* of National Maritime Polytechnic
- *Pre-need Plan Training* of Saint Peter Life Plans
- *Memorial Lot Selling Training* of Eternal Gardens
- *Traditional and Variable Insurance Training* of Manulife

NETWORK MARKETING COMPANIES

- Royale Business Club
- Goldlife
- JC Premiere
- UNO
- First Vita Plus
- VMobile Technologies
- Telepreneur Corporation
- JM Ocean Avenue
- Forever Living Products
- Usana
- Mary Kay
- Lifestyles Asia
- SWA
- AVON Cosmetics
- Dynapharm International
- Global Fusion
- Global Wealth Trade
- MonaVie
- Green Barley
- Direct Shopping
- Ever Bilena Cosmetics
- 4Life Research
- GNLD International
- Nikken Philippines
- QNet
- Sophie Paris
- Sundance
- Symmetry Global
- Tupperware Brands
- i-FERN
- Sante Barley
- The Filipino Dream
- AIM Global
- My Jinga Juice
- 1BRO
- Frontrow
- Organo Gold
- Amway
- Nu Skin
- Herbalife
- Max International
- GPRS
- Personal Collection
- DXN International
- CF Wellness
- ACT
- Sigma Wealth
- Dakki Classics
- Empower Marketing
- Filway Marketing
- GanoiTouch
- New Image
- Philkraft Wellness
- Reliv Philippines
- Stemtect
- Sunrider
- Tianshi Philippines
- Unicity Network

Reference: www.dsap.ph

FOREX MARKET BROKERS

- IronFX
- Instaforex
- HYMarket
- FXPro
- AvaTrade
- FXCM
- FXCC
- HotForex
- Easy Forex
- NordFX
- LiteForex
- FXopen
- Plus500
- Alpari
- Etoro
- ForexYard

Reference: www.forexbrokersaz.com/ph

SAVING AND COMMERCIAL BANKS

- Bank of the Philippine Islands
- Philippine National Bank
- Land Bank of the Philippines
- China Bank
- Union Bank
- United Coconut Planters Bank
- Development Bank of Philippines
- Philippine Bank of Communications
- Philippine Veterans Bank
- Standard Chartered Bank
- Citibank Philippines
- Philippine Business Bank
- Cooperative Banks
- Banco De Oro
- Metrobank
- Security Bank
- RCBC
- Maybank
- Philtrust Bank
- East West Bank
- Bank of Commerce
- Asia United Bank
- Robinsons Bank
- HSBC Philippines
- Thrift Banks
- Rural Banks

Reference: www.wikipedia.org

STOCK MARKET ONLINE BROKERS

- COL Financial Group Inc
- Unicapital Securities, Inc.
- AB Capital Securities
- Abacus Securities Corp
- Accord Capital Equities Corp
- First Metro Securities
- BA Securities, Inc
- Investors Securities, Inc.
- Optimum Securities Corp
- BPI Securities Corp
- DA Market Securities, Inc
- RCBC Securities, Inc
- Wealth Securities, Inc
- F.Yap Securities, Inc
- Angping & Associates
- Coherco Securities, Inc
- Maybank ATR Kim Eng Sec
- Regina Capital Dev Corp

Reference: www.pse.com.ph

UITF COMPANIES

- BDO Equity Fund
- PNB High Dividend Fund
- Best Balanced Fund (PBCom)
- Odyssey Balanced Fund(BPI)
- Diamond Fund (PBB)
- Infinity Peso Bond (EWB)
- ATRAM Peso Money Market
- Diversity Market Fund (BOC)
- BPI Equity Value Fund
- Rizal Equity Fund
- Gintong Sikap Secure (DBP)
- UnionBank Peso Balanced
- ABF Bond Index Fund (BPI)
- BDO Fixed Income Fund
- Rizal Dollar Bond Fund
- AUP Dollar Fund (PNB)

Reference: www.uitf.com.ph

MUTUAL FUND COMPANIES

- Philequity Fund,
- Philam Strategic Fund
- Sun Life Equity Fund
- Philippine Stock Index Fund
- GSIS Mutual Fund
- Cocolife Dollar Fund Builder
- GrepalifeFixed Income Fund
- BahayPariSolidaritas Fund
- NCM Mutual Fund of the Phil
- MAA Privilege Dollar Fixed Income Fund
- First Metro Equity Fund
- ATR Kim Eng Equity Fund
- United Fund, Inc.
- ALFM Growth Fund
- Optima Balanced Fund
- PAMI Asia Balanced Fund
- Prudentialife Fixed Fund
- Ekklesia Mutual Fund
- One Wealthy Nation Fund

Reference: www.pifa.com.ph

REAL ESTATE DEVELOPER COMPANIES

- Rockwell Land, Inc
- Vista Land and Lifescapes, Inc
- Eton Properties Philippines, Inc
- Century Properties Group, Inc
- SM Prime
- DMCI Homes
- Empire East Land Holdings
- Robinsons Land Corp
- Cityland Development Corp
- Double Dragon Properties Corp
- Euro Towers International, Inc
- Global Lands Develop & Invest Corp
- Greenfield Development Corp
- New San Jose Builders, Inc
- Ortigas & Company Partnership
- Philippine Sotheryby's International
- Picar Development
- RI Realty Developer Philippines Inc
- Federal Land, Inc
- Shang Properties
- Filinvest Land, Inc
- Ayala Land
- Megaworld
- Aboitiz Land
- Cathay Land, Inc
- Lica Land
- Landco Pacific
- Major Homes Inc
- Moldex Realty
- MRC Allied Inc
- Pro-Friends
- Avida Land
- SMDC
- Vicsal Properties
- Suntrust Properties

Reference: www.wikipedia.org

INSURANCE COMPANIES

- Manulife
- Insular Life
- Manulife Chinabank
- Pru Life UK
- PNB Life
- Great Life
- CLIMBS Life
- Paramount Life
- Philippine Prudential Life
- Cooperative Insurance System
- Country Bankers Life
- Sun Life
- Philippine Life
- Sunlife Grepa
- Phil AXA Life
- Generali Pilipinas
- First Life
- Beneficial Life
- Fortune Life
- Manila Bankers Life
- Philam Life
- Coco Life
- BPI Philam
- Pioneer Life
- AsianLife
- United Life
- Banclife
- Caritas Life
- BF Life
- CAP Life

Reference: www.insurance.gov.ph

PRE-NEED COMPANIES

- APEC
- Caritas Plans
- Destiny Plans
- Himlayang Pilipino
- Mercantile Care
- Provident Plans
- Transnational Plans
- AMA Plans
- Cityplans
- Eternal Plans
- Loyola Plans
- Paz Memorial
- St. Peter Plans
- Trusteeship Plans
- Ayala Plans
- Cocoplans
- First Union
- Manulife
- PhilPlans
- Sunlife Plan

Reference: www.insurance.gov.ph

CAR DEALERS

- Toyota
- Mitsubishi
- Hyundai
- Audi
- Ferrari
- Jaguar
- Dodge
- Land Rover
- Peugeot
- Lamborghini
- Chevrolet
- Nissan
- Isuzu
- Mercedes Benz
- Posche
- Chery
- Foton
- Mazda
- Subaru
- Volkswagen
- Honda
- Ford
- Kia
- BMW
- Maserati
- Chrysler
- Lexus
- Mini
- Suzuki
- Volvo

Reference: www.topgear.com.ph

HOW TO BECOME A MILLIONAIRE?

FRANCHISING BUSINESS

- 7-Eleven
- Aquabest
- Bobson
- FarmacianiDok
- Generika Drugstore
- Inkrite Refilling
- Penshoppe
- Plains and Prints
- Generics Pharmacy
- Andok's Food Corp
- Bread & Butter
- Chowking
- Dominos Pizza
- Fruit Magic
- Famous Belgian
- Hungry Juan
- LugawQueen
- Kenny Rogers
- Magnolia Chicken
- Max's Restaurant
- Mister Donut
- Pancake House
- Pinoy Ice Scramble
- Rai Rai Ken
- Slice N Dice
- Tokyo Tokyo
- The Aristocrat
- Bayad Center
- Bioessence Skin
- California Nails
- HBC
- PS Bank
- Manila Bulletin
- Electroworld Office
- Coca-Cola Bottlers
- Banana Peel Flip Flop
- Aficionado Perfume
- Bayo
- Celine
- Folded & Hung
- Islands Souvenirs
- Manels
- Picturebooks
- Toby's Sport
- 3M Pizza
- Bibingkinitan
- Cabalen
- Dimsum Break
- Figaro Coffee
- Fruitas
- Goodah!!!
- Happy Haus Donut
- Julie's Bakeshop
- Krispy Kreme
- Master Siomai
- Minute Burger
- Monterey Meatshop
- PansitMalabon
- Potato Corner
- Shakey's Pizza
- T.G.I. Friday's
- Teriyaki Boy
- The Coffee Beanery
- Yellow Cab Pizza
- Bluewater Day Spa
- Days Hotel
- Microtel Inns
- Reyes Haircutters
- Nestle Philippines
- Sarabia Optical
- The Philippine Star
- BPI Family Savings Bank
- Animaland
- Bench
- Family Mart
- Giordano
- Kamiseta
- Ministop
- Rustan's
- Vente
- Bigg's Diner
- Bo's Coffee
- Chic-Boy
- Dencio's
- Gotoking
- Goldilocks
- Greenwich
- Hap Chan
- Jollibee
- KFC
- MangInasal
- McDonalds
- Padi's Point
- Pier One
- Pizza Hut
- Red Ribbon
- Subway
- Tea 101
- Waffle Time
- Wendy's
- Flawless
- Netopia
- Mr. Quickie
- SeaOil
- Caltex
- Wave 89.1
- SGV & Co
- Happy Millionaire Book Shop
- Entrepreneur Philippines

Reference: www.pfa.org.ph

DISCLAIMER

The listed Investment Guide here is for reference purposes only and it is still your own responsibility to conduct your own research before any investment is to be conducted.

To the maximum extent permitted by the law, the author, the publisher and their respective affiliates disclaim any and all liability in the event that any information, analysis, ideas, advice or recommendations in the book prove to be inaccurate, incomplete or would result in any investment.

We'd like to hear from you! Send us your positive feedback so we can improve the Millionaire Book further. E-mail us at millionairebookauthor@gmail.com. Thank you!

Printed in Great Britain
by Amazon